D0166765

If Your Mind Wanders at Mass

THOMAS HOWARD

If Your Mind Wanders at Mass

IGNATIUS PRESS   SAN FRANCISCO

Original edition published by Franciscan University Press,
Steubenville, Ohio 43952
© 1995, Thomas Howard
All rights reserved
New edition printed by permission

Cover Art: *Prayer in the Garden of Gethsemane* (detail)
Fra Angelico
Museo San Marco, Florence, Italy
Scala / Art Resource, New York

Cover design by Roxanne Mei Lum

New edition published in 2001 by Ignatius Press, San Francisco
© 2000, Thomas Howard
All rights reserved
ISBN 978-0-89870-761-8
Library of Congress control number 99–73021
Printed in the United States of America ∞

Contents

Introduction

The Mass is the central act of Christian worship and has been so from the beginning. The earliest documents of the Church, written during the years just after the apostles died, record for us some of the very prayers that were then used at the eucharistic celebration when the believers gathered for worship.

It is worth noting that these people, most of whom were accustomed to synagogue worship, with its set readings and prayers, approached their newfound faith, with its startlingly new content (Jesus is our Messiah; he is Immanuel—God with us—and was born of the Virgin Mary, died and rose for us, ascended into heaven, and will come again), with great ardor and devotion, and yet with the solemnity to which they were accustomed from their old forms of worship, and which befitted the immense mysteries that had come upon them in the events of the Gospel.

I say "and yet", implying a possible disjuncture

between the ardor and devotion on the one hand and the solemnity on the other. It is often supposed that genuine ardor calls for spontaneity: that is, if we are wholehearted and fervent about something, the best way to register this is by giving voice, quite spontaneously, to whatever our heart feels at the moment. A lover, for example, will want to address his beloved with the unplanned immediacy that surges up from his heart and that tells her that what he is saying is indeed from his heart. By the same token, a Christian worshipper will want to give tongue to his own personal and genuine feelings of the moment when he speaks to the Savior in worship. Spontaneity would seem to be the very pledge and guarantor of authenticity here. Anything precast or rigidly structured would seem to imprison in a cage what ought to be free-flying, like a lark.

Indeed, this is all quite true. Spontaneity, not infrequently, gilds our most significant moments with its delightful guarantee of authenticity. What mother or father, for example, is not touched to the quick by the nosegay of limp dandelions, picked and proffered from the grimy little fist of their child. No bouquet arranged by the most celebrated floral artist can compete in these sweepstakes.

And yet this is not the whole story. It is an oddity about us mortals that when we come to the most profound experiences of our lives we become aware of the pale inadequacy of our own ability to respond with anything like an appropriately weighty response and find that we have to reach for something precast and structured.

For example: when a birth occurs. There is all the flurry of passing the word about and congratulating the parents and exclaiming over the happy event. But somehow we find that we want to do more. And so we all turn to that great treasure trove stored up by every tribe and culture and society, namely, tradition. Whether we are Watusi or Saxons or Jews or Celts, our traditions will offer to us some time-tested, public manner of giving shape to the event. For us in the West it may be the popping of champagne corks or the passing out of cigars. Certainly there will be cards, and flowers, and gifts—with pink or blue in evidence, according to whether the newborn is a girl or a boy. So dictates our tradition.

And no one supposes that because I offer a blue blanket for the bassinet of the new man-child my sentiments are other than heartfelt and fervent, even though I have been unabashedly *un*original in choosing blue. Blue is for boys: there it is.

Tradition. The precast. The structured. But nevertheless genuine.

Or marriage. Sometimes a young couple, in an effort to achieve a patina of authenticity about their marriage, will cobble up their own vows and invent little ceremonies that spring from their own private experience of having come to love each other. Such efforts can, at times, succeed, up to a point, and we, the well-wishers, may find ourselves touched.

But as often as not we are all plunged into embarrassment. We feel that we, the congregated friends, have been brought in to precincts where we have no business, as the couple gaze at each other, perhaps sing to each other in lyrics and tunes composed by one or the other of them, and exchange vows which, in an effort at truthfulness, blunder across the threshold that lies between the private and the public, forcing us all into the greatest possible anguish and discomfort.

And once again all tribes and cultures seem to have known instinctively that for the *public* marking of life's most profound events (birth, marriage, and death) we need something greater and sturdier than what our private attempts of the moment can gain. Whether it is ritual dances (with the very steps strictly choreographed by tradition), processions, ornate costumes, or ordeals, we find these events decked elaborately—and rigidly. In the West again, we dress the bride in white, with pearls, flowers, and a veil (this last has unhappily come upon great uncertainty, with the near disappearance of the notion of bride-as-virgin), and the groom in black and starched white. Slow, artificial stepping down the aisle. Attendants, also in elaborate costume, for the bride and groom. "Dearly beloved . . ." intoned by the minister. All very formal.

And all, somehow, exactly apt. For this is not just John and Mary deciding to take up residence together because they find each other attractive and congenial. It is the mystery of masculinity, this time embodied and enacted by John here, and the great mystery of femininity, here borne by Mary, coming together as man and woman have come together since Eden. Immemorial dignity crowns this man and this woman at this moment. The very mystery of our humanity itself, under its two modalities of masculine and feminine, arches in titanic splendor over their heads.

How shall we bespeak such immensities? My sentiments and yours are pitifully inadequate. We need the tradition springing from the ancient wellsprings of the race to come to our assistance and furnish us with words and movements that will give adequate shape to what it all *means*.

Likewise with death. This is "merely" a biological event (like birth and marriage). But we all know that biology is simply the tiny tip, under the species of mortal flesh, of the infinitely deep mystery of personhood. So when a human body ceases to breathe and live, we cannot leave the matter with simply disposing of the awkward residue. Nothing will do but ritual and ceremony, that is, words and movements, which, by virtue of themselves springing from the heart of the race, as it were, and of having been tested and dignified by ancient usage, have taken on the weight and solemnity that answer to the occasion, as opposed to our own helter-skelter attempts to respond to what has happened.

All of this brings us back around to the topic of worship. Worship belongs to the heart of the mystery to which our very existence as mortal men and women testifies. Once more, all tribes, cultures, and civilizations since the beginning have known that Something is to be invoked and propitiated. (Ironically, even those which, like Revolutionary France, or Stalinist Russia, have attempted to expunge the notion of a God to whom we owe our fealty, have had to make shift somehow to placate our unquenchable thirst for the transcendent by organizing huge spectacles, and rearing altars to Reason or to the Proletariat. Our inclination to worship is indestructible.)

Christianity teaches that this inclination is planted in us by the One for whom we were made, and by whom we were made, and to whom we go. It was to him that Abel offered sacrifice, and to him that Noah and Abraham and all of Israel raised altars. It was he who came among us at the Incarnation, and who wishes to be enthroned on the altar of our heart. It is he to whom Christian worship is addressed.

Since worship, along with the other central mysteries of our human existence, outstrips our own spontaneous attempts at responding adequately to the event at hand, we all find the help we need in words and movements handed down to us by wise tradition. Oh, to be sure, the Father whom we invoke is, like any father, delighted with whatever halting, lisping, stammering efforts we direct to him from our hearts. He does not sit as critic when we come to his knee. But when we come to the business of regular, recurrent, *public* worship, then we are glad for a form. A structure. The inexorable march of time, century after century, exhausts our spontaneity. We need a form.

Ancient Israel knew this, and hence the highly structured worship of the temple, and the texts of the Psalms. The newborn Church knew this, of course, and hence we find, as soon as she moved out from the morning of Pentecost into the long haul of history, that she gave a structure to her public worship.

Two properties attend recurring public occasions and hence are to be found in Christian worship. They are ritual and ceremony. Ritual refers to the words, and ceremony refers to the actions or movements.

In ritual we find what our spontaneity gropes for. The words, by a strange alchemy, transform our own leaden efforts into the gold of praise. *Te Deum laudamus, Te Dominum confitemur.* We praise thee, O God; we acknowledge thee to be the Lord. *Benedicite, omnia opera Domini.* O all ye works of the Lord, bless ye the Lord. *Magnificat anima mea.* My soul doth magnify the Lord.

If any tag end of suspicion still clouds our own ideas about ritual (precast words), we may recall our experience of singing. Happy birthday to you! We are glad to pour our own sentiments into that mold. "Amazing grace, how sweet the sound!" These words, written two hundred years ago by John Newton, somehow give us the very thing we grope for. Far from cramping us or stultifying our originality, the ritual words set us free and lead us out onto vistas immensely higher and more radiant than our own staggering phrases could have reached.

This is the reason for all that is written down in the prayer books and missals used in Christian worship. As we make our own voice one with the immemorial voice of the Church, we find that we are caught up into something much bigger than the tiny pool of our own resources. *Gloria in excelsis Deo! Sanctus! Sanctus! Sanctus!* Who will want to interrupt here with his own poor notions?

It is the same with ceremony. Non-Catholic Christians often wonder what the bobbing up and down, and turning this way and that, is all about. It looks like mumbo-jumbo.

But of course any activity can look like mumbo-jumbo to the uninitiated. Tennis itself, or a rugby match, or a military parade, or a wedding: What are they all doing, moving this way and that?

As one comes to know what is at stake in the movements, one can see the point. We mortals, for example, all seem to know that getting down onto our knees somehow is a movement which bespeaks something true about ourselves and the deity before whom we find ourselves. Pagans and

Christians alike know this. Courtesy teaches a man to stand up when a woman enters the room. Court etiquette teaches men to bow and women to curtsy when the sovereign enters. We are ceremonial creatures. Navajo rain dances, the Highland fling, flamenco, Viennese waltzes: movement—formal, exact movement—seems to belong to our dignity as human beings. It carries an enormous freight of significance.

In the Mass we see these elements of ritual and ceremony, which belong so profoundly to our humanness, brought into the service of God Most High. It is worth remembering, in this connection, that we mortals do not ceremonialize events by way of escaping from them, as though to throw up a smoke screen. The opposite is the truth: we turn to ceremony when we know that we are encountering something—birth, or death—which eludes our mere cognitive grasp, but which calls for some response from us. Indeed, what turns out to be the case is that, far from skirting or beclouding the issue, the ceremony vouchsafes the significant event to us in a way that no other approach quite satisfies. The wedding procession or the funeral obsequies are not there to blur the event; rather, they supply us with a shape, as it were, for our otherwise somewhat unruly emotions.

In this connection it might also be helpful to speak of music, which has always attended the worship of God. The Mass is the Mass, of course, with or without music. No splendid organ or English boys' choir can make the Mass *more* what it is. On the other hand, since we are physical creatures and not disembodied intellects, our beings cry out often for music. We turn to music when we are happy (some twinkling scherzo movement of a Mozart flute concerto) or sad (the "Pathétique" sonata) or maudlin ("Auld Lang Syne"). It belongs to our humanness.

The Church has embraced music and pressed it into service as she has accepted all the other aspects of our humanness (painting, sculpture, architecture, weaving, smithying). One of the most ancient modes under which we hear music in connection with Christian worship is Gregorian chant. Chant is perhaps the most austere setting for texts. There is very little in chant to appeal to mere sensuality or frivolity. The spare discipline of the sequence of tones has the effect of purging the text of any histrionics (fortissimo, pianissimo; largo, vivace) and of setting it up the way a Tiffany setting sets up a diamond: one is obliged to fix one's attention on the diamond itself. Psalmody sung to the Gregorian tones is an acquired taste, like a very dry wine (as opposed to fruit punch). But those who have become accustomed to it will testify that there is no other musical setting for texts which achieves quite the pellucid purity offered by chant.

Renaissance polyphony (the music of Byrd, Palestrina, Gabrieli, or Gibbons) is another genre of music encountered in churches and cathedrals which can afford a trained choir. The settings for the Kyrie, Gloria, Credo, Sanctus and Benedictus, and Agnus Dei from this period (sixteenth and seventeenth centuries) are almost unbearably beautiful. It is always a risk to make sweeping musical judgments, but the Church does seem to recognize that the choral music from this period caught something that can only be called "true". Whereas later centuries at times tend toward the theatrical, or the soaringly sentimental, or the frivolous when it comes to sacred music, the Renaissance more often than not seems able to evoke sempiternal ineffabilities in its music with fitting tact and solemnity.

Hymnody is always a problematic topic. The Church has discovered and brought into use some of the immense treasury of Protestant hymns and has found them to be invigorating. There is also a very rich trove of hymnody from the first thousand years of the Church, translated from the Latin into English by the nineteenth-century Anglican priest John Mason Neale, especially hymns for the feasts of the liturgical year. These have not yet come into general use in the Catholic Church, but only good would result from their use. In recent decades there has been an avalanche of "praise songs" of varying quality. Insofar as many of them are scriptural, they may turn out to be lasting. Others—a great many others—bear the particular stamp of sentiments abroad during the 1970s and 1980s, and are thereby dated, and perhaps could be sequestered with very little loss to the enterprise of Christian worship.

One last note. Many Catholics, especially converts from denominations where dignity of worship and elegant music have been specialties, have difficulty when they find themselves at a Mass where all the ends seem frayed: crying babies, restless (and to all appearances bored) worshippers, feeble congregational singing, maladroit accompaniment from guitars or electronic organ, and, in some cases, a celebrant who may see his task primarily to be one of stirring up bonhomie among the gathered people by means of a happy demeanor and a running set of interpolations and asides added to the words in the missal. The great thing to be kept firmly in mind here is that one meets God Most High in the liturgy, and God Most High did have a way of being found in the most unlikely spots: wind, a blazing shrub, the voice of a donkey, a tent in the desert of Sinai, and in a stable. Nazareth was the ultimate small town (read dull). And yet, and yet . . . It is salutary to keep one's personal tastes and preferences on a very short rein in the precincts of the Eucharist. It is holy ground, stable or no stable. Mass celebrated on the hood of a jeep with shells bursting all around is as much the Mass as the liturgy celebrated in Saint John Lateran by the Bishop of Rome himself.

Part One

What Is the Mass?

I

The Center of Christian Life

At the very center of the Christian life we find the Mass. All the other aspects of this life—prayer, the reading of the Bible, works of charity, fasting— and all the other sacraments come into bright focus in the Mass.

But what is it, this Mass? The fact that the Church has never settled upon one single term for this rite—we call it "Eucharist" and "Holy Communion" and "The Lord's Supper"—suggests straight off something of the rich depths which we encounter when we assist at Mass.

"Assist at": that is an old and very accurate way of referring to our attendance at Mass. We are not spectators. We are not an audience. We are the congregation, brought together (congregated) to *do* something—all of us, not solely the priest up there at the altar. Every one of us who wants to be numbered among "the faithful" is, by virtue of his baptism, made to be a sharer in the priesthood of Jesus Christ. The priest himself, by virtue of his ordination, participates in that priesthood in a particular way. He is "ordained" to preside at the Lord's Table, that is, to be in the place of Jesus Christ, who instituted this sacrament when he broke the bread and blessed the cup at the Last Supper. But we the faithful share in the action by uniting ourselves to the Sacrifice of Jesus Christ which is made present in the Mass, and by offering our adoration, and our very selves, *and* all our work and our joys and our sufferings, and our aspirations, to God as the particular things which we alone can offer. No one else can offer *me* to the Lord. This is an act which I alone can carry out.

But we have come a long way in one paragraph. Every clause and every phrase of what we have just read opens out onto immense regions of mystery. To learn all of it, or even the tenth part of it, is the work of a lifetime and more. The greatest saints and mystics—Saint Thomas Aquinas himself, or Saint Teresa of Avila—would on their deathbeds protest that they had scarcely come near the outer precincts of the mysteries brought to us in the Mass.

We know this, of course. We all know that every single detail of the liturgy—every word spoken, every gesture on our part as well as on the priest's, every vessel and detail of the furnishings and of the vestments, nay, and of the whole church itself—is freighted with meaning, and that to glimpse even one fugitive aspect of the mysteries is often all we can manage. And we find that, insofar as we do occasionally glimpse something clearly, we feel ourselves to be hailed with glories so thunderous that, like the Israelites at Sinai when they heard the great horn signaling God's presence, we want to cry out for shelter from this awesome Presence.

But of course such moments of stark awareness come to us only seldom, and briefly. For most of us, most of the time, it is all a matter of doing our duty in simple obedience to the Lord's charge to us, "Do this in remembrance of me." Oh, to be sure, we often feel that we have been blessed; and not infrequently we find consolation, or instruction, or encouragement, or rebuke, in the reading and preaching of the Scriptures, and sustenance for our lives in the Body and Blood on which we feed. All of this comes to us day by day, or week by week, as we assist at Mass. But to grasp the full significance of it, all at once, however: this we can never do in this mortal life. We are not yet ready to bear the "weight of glory" hinted at in the liturgy.

But insofar as we make it our practice to come expectantly, and to participate attentively, and to respond obediently to all that the liturgy proclaims and makes present, we will find that we are indeed well on "the Way" (this is what the early Christians called the Christian life) and that our whole being is gradually but steadily drawing nearer to that joy for which we were created in the first place, and which we forfeited when we, in our Father Adam and our Mother Eve, made our grab for something we felt should be *ours* (and not thine, O Lord). In the liturgy we begin to learn to give back—to offer—to God that which is his in any case: that is, ourselves and our world.

The following are the reflections of a lay Christian believer on the great mystery of the Eucharist. The saints and doctors of the Church and the Magisterium have opened up the vista and have spoken to us authoritatively on the matter. These reflections are one itinerary in that vista. For every point made, a thousand more would not suffice to encompass the mystery. But we (lay Christians) may hope to see this and that as we travel, and what we see is worth reflecting on.

2

Go. The Mass Is Finished

The Mass. What does that word mean? It is probably the most common term for the Church's worship, and every Catholic can use the word without giving it a second thought.

The word is an English shortening and adaptation of the Latin dismissal which the priest pronounced over the congregation at the end of the Mass: *Ite, missa est*. Roughly it means "Go, the Mass is finished."

That might seem a somewhat chilling term to be adopted by the whole Church to signify its worship. Why funnel the thing down to the dismissal? That's when we leave worship behind, surely?

No. Those words touch on one of the richest mysteries of the Christian life, namely, that we, all of us believers, having been made "priests" at our baptism, are appointed (as every priest is appointed) to offer sacrifice, and to offer it daily and continuously. That is, in our baptism we have "crossed over" from the land where we were our own masters to the kingdom where we, as servants of the King, may offer ourselves and our whole work to him daily. In doing this, we "hallow" (make holy) all that we offer: namely, everything. Nothing is secular for a Christian (or ought not to be, shall we say). All belongs to the Lord, all is set apart for him: all is holy.

All of this is clear during the Mass. In that one hour of the week (or of the day if we are fortunate enough to be able to assist at Mass daily) we are conscious of "offering" everything to the Lord. All the words and actions of the Mass bid us do this. The ritual and the ceremony give us the structures that enable us to make our offering, whereas, left to our own private resources and inclinations, we would probably give up the attempt as too daunting.

But: "Go, the Mass is finished." This means, not "OK. You have discharged your weekly obligation. Now go live your Monday through Saturday as you wish, then come back and worship for another hour." Rather it means "Go—and carry with you, out of this church into your daily routines, all that you have meant and done here." That is, here in the Mass you knelt before the Lord, and by your gestures you placed yourself under his Cross (you crossed yourself how many times?), and you spoke words which declared your readiness to obey his Word, and you partook of the Great Offering itself when you received the Host and sipped from the Cup. What did all that mean?

Well, among other things it identified you as his child, his servant, his priest; and as such you identified yourself as someone who is prepared to make his whole life (household chores, driving in traffic, sitting in committees, doing schoolwork or factory work, being with your family and friends) an offering to God, which is what we human beings were created to do. You are not your own. Your work is not your own. Your world is not your own. It all belongs to the Most High; and our highest dignity as *Homo sapiens* is to "return" it all to him as an oblation, consciously, volitionally, intelligently. The rest of creation praises him ceaselessly: the north wind, the surf, the cirrus clouds, the gazelles and dolphins and fireflies, and the sweetness of raspberries and the gold of ripe wheat and the song of the winter wren—this all praises him inarticulately, and inevitably. You and I, the heirs of Adam and Eve, are to be the stewards and

lords of this creation, offering it and ourselves back
to the Lord, who made it all and who gave it to us.

What you are doing in the Mass is focusing,
bringing to a sharp, bright point, what you are to
do every minute of your lives, namely, making
your offering. There is nothing you do during the
Mass that you are not to be doing every day and
every hour of the week. Oh, to be sure, you can't
be thinking every moment, "Lord, I offer this to
you." You have to get on with your life and work.
But by recurring and frequent aspirations (little
prayers or exclamations to God) you should be
consciously making your offering to God of whatever you are doing or whatever you are undergoing. And undergirding these brief, conscious acts
there should be growing in you a more and more
profound consciousness of the duty and dignity
which is yours as his child and servant, of returning all to him.

At the high point of every Mass we find our
cue, as it were. For there we find ourselves both in
the Upper Room at the Last Supper and also, in a
mystery, at Calvary. Here is where the Son of God,
the Second Adam (representing us all), the Savior,
the *Agnus Dei* declared and made his spotless offering *in our behalf.* We can add nothing, no whit or
jot, to this offering of his. It was, as one ancient

rite phrases it, "a full, perfect, sufficient Sacrifice, Oblation, and Satisfaction, for the sins of the whole world". Our sins had cut us off from God. His offering makes the forgiveness of our sins possible, and thus restores us to God's presence, where we may once again stand and make offering to him.

This is why the Church speaks of our "uniting ourselves" with the sacrifice of Jesus Christ on the Cross. We can't bring anything of our own. We have no entry into the Holy of Holies where God dwells without the cleansing Blood of Jesus, who is the perfect Lamb of sacrifice. Insofar as we make any offering, it must be united with his offering in order to be made acceptable to God. And this is why the Mass is the focal point—quite literally, the "focusing"—of our whole day or week. Here we declare and do, consciously and articulately and ceremonially, what we should be doing all week long, namely, praising him and worshipping him with the offering of our songs, our prayers, and our innermost intentions and aspirations.

That is a great deal to extract from the one syllable "Mass". But it is all there. Go, says the Church, and let there be no rupture between what you have said and done in this hour and what you say and do for the other hours of your week. Here is the pattern. Here is the cue. Here is the whole truth of your life, concentrated, focused, clarified. Go.

The Mass would be sterile and futile if it were locked and sealed inside one magic hour of the week. Like Calvary itself, the whole point of it is that it "overflow". Our Lord's life (his Blood) was poured out, spilled onto the ground; and, says faith, from the soil on Golgotha it spread to cover the whole earth. Just so, you and I take our own place at Calvary so that our whole life may be spilled as an oblation to God *for the life of the world*. "I am crucified with Christ", exclaims Saint Paul, and the Church has always heard his words as applying to every believer. During the Mass we declare this and enact it ceremonially. But the ceremony becomes a farce if it is locked inside this one hour. It must overflow into our week. Go, says the Church. You are sent. *Ite, missa est.*

3

Liturgy: The Work of the People

In recent years the word *liturgy* has come into common usage among Christians. It can refer to the Liturgy of the Hours, which is set forth for the whole Church (laity as well as religious and clergy) by Paul VI. This is made clear in his November 1970 apostolic constitution *The Canticle of Praise*, promulgating the Divine Office, and also in the *General Instruction on the Liturgy of the Hours*, in which the laity especially is urged to enter anew into the rich and ancient habit of daily prayer in common with the whole Church. (See also the *Catechism of the Catholic Church*, 1066–73.)

But the word *liturgy* refers especially to the Mass. It comes from a Greek word that means literally "the work of the people". In what sense is the Mass the work of the people? What people?

To take the second part of the question first, this

"people" is us—the Church—Christians—the people of God. Of course there is one profound sense in which the whole human race is God's people, since he made us and since Christ died for us all. And there is a more restricted sense in which the Jews, who were chosen from all the ancient tribes to be in a particular sense God's people, may be called the people of God. But the Church, following the writings of Saint Paul, understands herself to be the heir of the Jews and to be the "new Israel". So, in this usage, the Church speaks of herself as the people of God: those bound together by a common faith in Jesus Christ, the Messiah.

But what is this "work of the people"? It is a manifold work, entailing the totality of our lives, of course; but the particular work of the liturgy is the offering of sacrifice. When we come together for the liturgy, our identity as God's priestly people is especially apparent. Again, there are priests (presbyters) called from among us to preside at the liturgy; and the Church teaches that theirs is a unique service, partaking in Christ's High Priesthood in a way not true of the laity, who are nonetheless in some sense priests by virtue of their baptism.

A priest offers sacrifice. We mortals, the heirs of

Adam and Eve, were created to offer the continual sacrifice of adoration, and of the fruit of our work, and of our very selves to the Most High. At the Fall we withheld part of that sacrifice: we wished to seize things as our own rather than as God's. In so doing, we brought ruin down on our heads and on the whole creation, and it was only the sacrifice of the Son of God himself on the Cross which has saved us and the whole universe from final ruin. His is *the* Sacrifice, anticipated in Israel by the lambs slain at the Passover when God freed his people from their slavery in Egypt. The *Catechism* speaks of this sacrifice this way: "When the Church celebrates the Eucharist, she commemorates Christ's Passover, and it is made present: the sacrifice Christ offered once for all on the cross remains ever present" (*Catechism of the Catholic Church*, 1364; cf. Heb 7:25–27).

Our sacrifice of worship and praise, and of ourselves, to God in the liturgy is offered *in union with* the sacrifice of Jesus Christ. Left to ourselves, we are not worthy to offer anything at all to God. We forfeited that dignity at the Fall. But restored in Jesus Christ to communion with God, we may "come boldly unto the throne of grace", as the Letter to the Hebrews (4:16) phrases it, bringing with us the Blood of Jesus. The Church teaches that there is one sacrifice, one altar, and one priest-hood: Jesus himself. What we in the Church, priests and laity, enact is a participation in that sacrifice.

There is an ancient idea, familiar to the Jews and to the Orthodox Church, that we mortals were made to "bless" God, that is, to give thanks and praise to him for the perfections of his own being and for all his works in creation. It is our particular dignity as men consciously, intelligently, and volitionally to "bless" him for all of his gifts and, as it were, to lead the praises of all creatures. This is the way of putting what this work of the people is in the liturgy.

The word *Eucharist*, which, like the word *liturgy*, has come into more frequent use in the years since Vatican II, particularly stresses this work of "bless-ing" God. Eucharist means "thanksgiving". As the Lord Jesus gave thanks at the Last Supper, so we join in that act at the Eucharist. We especially thank God for his great works in creation, re-demption, and sanctification, that is, in making us and the world, in saving (redeeming) us and the world, and in making us holy so that we will be fit to stand in his presence and serve him forever.

The expressions "the Lord's Supper" and "the Breaking of Bread" stress the connection between what we do at Mass and the Last Supper. The altar, which recalls the Cross, is also a table. You feast at a table, and Christians proclaim that they feast at Mass. We believe that we are fed, in a mystery, with the very Body and Blood of the Lord Jesus, as he taught us in the sixth chapter of John's Gospel: "My flesh is food indeed, and my blood is drink indeed. . . . He who eats me will live because of me" (Jn 6:55, 57). From the beginning the Church has taken his words utterly seriously: we have no warrant to drain out the significance of those words and to decide that they are only symbolic. There is no scandal in a symbol; but when he spoke those mysterious words in John 6, many of his hearers were so offended at his refusal to ease things by admitting that he was speaking only symbolically that they left him. The Church has always heard his words as meaning what they say. In fact, the early Christians found themselves accused of cannibalism when their pagan neighbors found out that they believed they were actually partaking of Christ's Body and Blood at their worship.

Another phrase sometimes used for the Mass is "Holy Communion", although ordinarily when we use this phrase we refer to the particular act of eating the Host and drinking from the Cup. This draws on the "supper" aspect of the mysteries that are enacted at Mass and emphasizes that "by this sacrament we unite ourselves to Christ, who makes us sharers in his Body and Blood to form a single body" (*Catechism of the Catholic Church*, 1331; cf. 1 Cor 10:16–17).

In this Communion we are united with Jesus Christ, and with each other as fellow members of his one Body, and also with the whole Church, including all the people of God who have gone before us. The Church believes that the Savior, by his Resurrection, overcame the great barrier of death and united *all* of his people—those still in pilgrimage here on earth and those who have died. This is the famous "communion of saints" on which we count so earnestly when we pray. The Church teaches that, in a mystery, the veil hanging between time and eternity is drawn back, as it were, in the liturgy, and that we really are one worshipping body "with angels and archangels, and the whole company of heaven" (Preface for Epiphany).

It is an awesome picture, and one that may frequently spur us to renewed ardor if our attention wanders at Mass, or if our spirits droop from fatigue, preoccupation, or general lassitude.

4

Heavenly Worship

If we pay attention to each step of the Mass, both
the words given to us from Scripture and tradition
and the ceremonial gestures asked of us, we will
discover that we have been brought into a region
far, far greater than the very small region encom-
passed by our own powers of thought, imagination, and devotion. The touchstone in the liturgy
is not first of all *my* immediate needs, preoccupa-
tions, or feelings. We are bidden, quite literally,
into the immense vista hinted at in the book of
Hebrews thus: "You have come to Mount Zion
and to the city of the living God, the heavenly
Jerusalem, and to innumerable angels in festal gathering" (Heb 12:22).

These are august precincts, and by far the best
demeanor here is that demeanor enjoined on
Peter when he gabbled busily on the Mount of

Transfiguration: silence and attentiveness. My agenda can come presently, to be sure: we are urged by the Most High to unburden ourselves—of even the most trivial concerns—when we come to the Throne of Grace, which appeared in Ezekiel's vision as sapphire (cf. Ezek 1:26). But when we come to this throne in the liturgy, that is, in the corporate act which joins us with the entire people of God, everywhere and always, and with the host of heaven, we dispose ourselves accordingly. Like the Jews in ancient Israel, we find that words and actions prescribed by hallowed public usage answer far more adequately here than our own subjective efforts, much as our gracious Lord and Father invites just such efforts. And we find a paradox: the great tumble and clutter of our own concerns, lo and behold, comes to rest here. It finds the very place it sought in its rush. It appears in its proper context, namely, as part of that which is taken into the mystery of Calvary and transfigured.

It is a salutary thing to keep clearly in our minds, as we assist at the liturgy, the distinction between the public and the private. Efforts are often undertaken, in some sectors of Christendom, to achieve "spontaneity" in public worship. We want our worship to be real; we want it to express what we are feeling; we want to avoid the rote and the precanned, which stifle true worship, surely?

Not altogether, says the ancient Church. Spontaneity is a wholesome thing in its appropriate place. But when we mortals come to the great and profound events which mark our existence (birth, marriage, and death, for example), we find that our own resources fail us. We grope for words. We fumble for some footing. We want a frame strong enough to sustain and order these immense experiences. This is why every tribe, culture, society, and civilization in every century has set its experience into ceremonial form. We are ceremonial creatures. Our whole being yearns for the solemnity and durability and massiveness of ceremony. We are not, as the Gnostics and Manichaeans wished, mere souls imprisoned in clay bodies. The lecture format for worship so sedulously preserved by the Reformation churches does not correspond to all that we are. We cry out to kneel. Our noses, surely the least auspicious of our members, cry out to join our voices and our thoughts and our knees in worship: hence incense.

All of this is bespoken in the specifically public (corporate) nature of the Mass. This is not just me at my private prayers (I should come to Mass *from* those prayers; or remain afterward, if only for a few moments, for those prayers). Now I dispose myself as one member of an immeasurable throng, which is present, says the Church, at every single celebration of the Eucharist, even though there may be only me, some old and holy crone, and the priest present in this church building at the moment. But again, paradoxically, my finding myself as one in a throng does not override or obliterate the full mystery and depth of my own personhood and individuality: lo and behold, I find that this *I* is more utterly at home and more intimately addressed by the "Thou" whom my soul seeks than in any other moment. I am not a statistic here. My God, my Father, my Savior, my soul's Love comes to me here and calls me by my own name.

The liturgy as it took shape in the decades following Pentecost, at the hands of the apostles and then of the men on whom they laid their hands to be shepherds (bishops), and as it developed organically through the centuries, presents us with a map of reality, so to speak. Nay: more than a map. It unfurls what is true, and displays it to our gaze, and makes it present to us. That is no empty word or mere figure of speech, that "makes it present". When the Lord told his disciples, "Do this for a remembrance of me", the word he used (*anamnesis*) denotes a remembering which is *a making present*. What we have in the Mass, says the ancient Church, is not simply a recalling of events-gone-by (which is the idea at work in the Christian denominations which take their cues from the sixteenth-century Swiss reformer Ulrich Zwingli: he insisted, as over against the universal testimony of the Church from the Fathers on down, that the bread and wine remain simply symbols, and that there is no "mystery", at least in this matter of the "elements"). Somehow, says the Church, in this act we find that the scrim between time and eternity, or between earth and heaven, or between the seen and the unseen, has been drawn back; we really are in a mystery (the word "sacrament" is the Latin translation for the Greek *mysterion*)—we really are at the Lord's own table, like the disciples in the Upper Room; and at the cross, with Mary and John; and with the angels and archangels and the whole company of saints among whom we place ourselves when we sing "Holy, holy, holy".

In these precincts, again, we scarcely know what to say. We may well take our cue from Moses and Gideon and Isaiah and Zechariah and Joseph and Paul here, who, when they found that scrim drawn back and themselves hailed by the angel of the Lord, were fearful. That is a salutary attitude with which to begin. But then to us, as to them, is spoken the divine "Fear not." We may indeed come "boldly", as Saint Paul instructs us; but that does not mean hastily, or foolishly, or busily. The words and actions of the liturgy are like our script. Here is how it is done in these heavenly courts. Join in. So says the heavenly throng. So says the Church. The sequence proposed here of acclamations, prayers, confession, Scriptures, praises, consecrations, and charges is, you will find, a sequence which answers flawlessly to the shape of your mortal life and of your identity as person and of the redemption and glorification of this person. It was not thought up in an hour. It stands at a polar extreme from the random, the ad hoc, and the "creative". What we do not want here is Tom, Dick, or Harry's notions of the moment, affecting as those notions might be. We need the language and deportment of heaven.

Let us look at this map. Or rather, let us listen to the bidding into the Holy of Holies which the liturgy constitutes.

Part Two

The Order of the Mass

5

Introductory Rites

Entrance Song

The liturgy begins with the Entrance Song—what used to be called the Introit—also known as the Entrance Antiphon. This is a text from Scripture which may be sung by the choir or spoken by the celebrant. It strikes the note, so to speak, for this day's liturgy. It anticipates the themes that we will encounter in the readings from Scripture and that belong to this day in the Church's year. On special feasts and memorials—say, in Lent, or at Christmas, or on a feast of the Blessed Virgin or one of the saints—this Entrance Song will bespeak the occasion. On the days of Ordinary Time (the long stretch from Pentecost to Advent) on which no particular feast occurs, our attention is turned to the theme presented to us by the readings. A great part of the Church year is taken up with mere, sheer instruction in the faith. The whole of Scripture is opened up for us and proposed for our contemplation and obedience. The Entrance Song hails us and bids us attend. It corrals our helter-skelter thoughts, as it were, and orders them to the theme for this day's liturgy.

Greeting

Then, making the sign of the Cross, the priest salutes us with the formula which must be inscribed over everything we do, and most especially over what we do in the liturgy: "In the name of the Father, and of the Son, and of the Holy Spirit." Also making the sign of the Cross, we respond, "Amen."

The gulf between hell and heaven has suddenly appeared here, and we have placed ourselves on the side of heaven.

If that seems too overblown an idea to attach to such a routine formula, we may recall that this formula, so apparently commonplace, does two things: it invokes the ineffable splendor of the Most High himself in his triune majesty, and it places those who utter it under his reign. Hell cannot speak this formula. Hell hates it. Everything in me that is reminiscent of hell—all haughtiness, and vanity, and malice, and venality, and cravenness and pusillanimity and concupiscence—quails before this invocation. By an act of my intelligence and my will I serve notice to my own innermost being and to hell and its minions that I wish to be found in the court of this heavenly Sovereign, where nothing but holiness is admitted.

It is a formula not to be spoken lightly. It opens out upon the liturgy for us where, by word and ceremony, we begin to taste and to learn how to behave in heaven. But hell may not enter here.

Because this is so daunting a situation, we mortals so desperately in need of salvation are immediately encouraged with the following: "The grace of our Lord Jesus Christ and the love of God and the fellowship of the Holy Spirit be with you all" or "The Lord be with you." We answer, "And also with you." your spirit.

Ah. This Holy Trinity, so unimaginable, so exalted, and so terrifying to all in us that might wish to escape him, greets us with "grace . . . love . . . fellowship."

These are no longer the precincts of terror for us. The liturgy bids us into grace and love and fellowship. Once again (and the liturgy has scarcely begun) we find ourselves summoned into the company of saints—understood not as a region utterly remote from our workaday world, but rather as that very world redeemed, raised, and glorified. We who come to this rite and assist at it are to live this day, down here on this earth, in that grace, love, and fellowship. Or put it the other way around: that grace and love and fellowship touch, nay suffuse, and therefore glorify, our ordinariness—the "prayers, works, joys, and sufferings of this day", as the Morning Offering puts it. It opens onto the vision of heaven, as over against the futility and ennui and insupportable weariness that mark human life lived without this vision.

The liturgy is a good tutor. That is, it teaches us what is to be said, day by day, by the Christian soul, rather than leaving us mired in the bog of our own resources and feelings, so sadly inadequate as they are. The worship of the Church opens out for us what we *ought* to say rather than asking us what we *feel* like saying.

Penitential Rite

On certain occasions there may follow here the rite of blessing and sprinkling of holy water. This rite presents to us in a vivid way a reminder of the water of our baptism, which washed away our sins, and of the living water of salvation, which was promised to us by Jesus Christ. As rain sprinkles the earth and makes it fructify, so the fountain of salvation showers upon us day by day with this living water. The rite of sprinkling makes this present to us who are gathered here as a local case in point of the whole of redeemed humanity.

On most days, however, the Penitential Rite follows the greeting. The priest bids us prepare for the approaching celebration of the paschal mystery by calling to mind our sins and acknowledging them.

This is one of the few places in the Mass where the focus is turned on me. It is not a particularly flattering turning of attention; to prepare ourselves to celebrate the sacred mysteries, we do not say, "How good I am!" but "I have sinned."

This will no doubt seem obsequious or even masochistic to people who have been suckled only on modern ideas of self-affirmation and whose notion of freedom is to "feel good" about themselves. But Christians, along with the Jews of ancient Israel, know that this strait gate and narrow way asks us who enter upon it to submit our innermost being to the searchlight of the divine holiness and to make a clean breast of all the duplicity and egoism and self-will that lurks in us and energizes so many—nay, all—of our attitudes and words and acts. I have sinned, and it is by acknowledging this that I can find myself at the foot of the Cross. Christians know that this way leads directly out toward true freedom and health ("salvation" means health, actually).

The people who sup with God at his table are, to a man, forgiven people. No saint is there on any other basis. The Virgin Mary alone knew from the beginning what it was to be a completely whole person, unstained by the sin that mars the image of God in us. The rest of us, right on up to Teresa and Francis and Thomas, arrive with "I have sinned" on our lips. If in fact this is the truth about us (and Scripture makes it clear that it is), then facing and owning that truth will make us free. Here in this company there need be no furtive and hugger-mugger concealing of squalid and embarrassing little (or big) truths about ourselves. In private confession we may itemize all of it to God, and in the sacrament of Reconciliation, when we have done just this in the presence of his minister the priest, our ears may hear the great, liberating "I absolve you." There is no other prescription for human freedom. And, says the liturgy, there is no other footing upon which we may enter the mysteries which we have gathered to enact.

In some cases this penitential rite will take the form of an explicit confession ("I confess to almighty God, and to you my brothers and sisters, that I have sinned through my own fault"). Often it will take the form of the priest invoking the Lord ("You were sent to heal the contrite. . . . You came to call sinners. . . . You plead for us . . ."), with us repeating, "Lord, have mercy." We then hear from the priest's lips the words of absolution: "May almighty God have mercy on us, forgive us our sins. . . ."

Once more, routine words. We become accustomed to them by hearing them again and again over the years, yet they open up staggering vistas for us if we pay attention. All myths and legends, and all poetry and art and music, testify to the fathomless yearning of us mortals to find and to come into touch with the gods: if only some word would be spoken to us from the silence. But this yearning is shot through with fear: Who might the god be? Will he crush us? What ought we to do to appease his just wrath (we know we have not done well in his eyes, surely)? One can see in the stony expressionlessness of the gods seated in remote majesty in Egyptian sculpture, rebuffing all possible approaches, our deep-seated fear of them and our awareness of our ruinous inadequacy before them. We may see something similar in the bearded gods of Assyria. And how do we stay on the good side of Zeus, capricious and mercurial as he is? If only we could *know* them, and find our way into their good graces.

We can. The god—*the* God—came to us with skins to cover our poor nakedness in Eden, and in the rainbow, and in the burning bush, and in the poignant words of the prophets ("O my people . . ."), and finally in the Annunciation. Comfort ye, comfort ye, my people, says this God. My name is Jesus—Savior. I bring not terror and doom but tidings of great joy. Your sins are forgiven.

We hear all of this in the words of absolution. This is the One whom we gather to adore, or rather who has gathered us with his gracious "Come and dine." No wonder we answer "Amen" to such comforting words as the absolution utters.

Kyrie

There now follows the Kyrie eleison (Lord, have mercy), unless these words have been used in the preceding act of penance.

To some non-Catholic Christians this seems like an odd thing to repeat. Hasn't God already had mercy on us when he came in his Son for our salvation? Why go on with this sort of petition? It makes it sound as though we are not sure of our God.

The answer which we hear the liturgy itself give is that in this threefold address to the Lord we both acclaim him ("Kyrios!" was one of the greetings for an emperor in the ancient world) and acknowledge that it is only insofar as he does, always, "have mercy on us" that we stand at all. None of us may appear in these precincts on any other footing. Thus the Kyrie is not a sort of hopeless plucking at his garments, a kind of timorous pawing of his arm, coaxing God to be nice to us. Rather, it comes from our profound confidence that he *has* had mercy, he *does* have mercy, he *will* have mercy. And there is as much a note of exultation in the acclamation as there is of supplication.

The Kyrie also reminds us of a special character of the liturgy, namely, that in all of its parts we find both a sequence and a simultaneity. That is, we move "through" the drama of our redemption step by step: but also, at each step, we proclaim and enact something which is ever present and always true. We don't "leave behind", say, the grace of our Lord Jesus Christ and the love of God. To be sure, we move on from it in the sequence of our words and actions in the liturgy; but in each acclamation, prayer, or canticle we bespeak that which is perpetually and unchangingly true. When we cry "Kyrie!" we both ask for the Lord's mercy on us (which we need) and also declare something that constitutes part of the very architecture of God's temple in heaven.

There is yet another point worth marking here. In the Kyrie, especially when it is set in the polyphony of a Tomás Luis de Victoria or a Palestrina, we may hear the fathomless cry of the whole race of man ascending to heaven from the depths. Kyrie! goes up from all widows, and all dispossessed and brutalized children, and from all the maimed, and the prisoners and exiles, and from every sickbed, and indeed from all wounded beasts, and, we could believe, from all rivers and seas stained with man's filth and landscapes scarred by his plunder. In the liturgy, somehow, we stand before the Lord *in behalf of* his whole groaning creation. And beyond the liturgy: when we hear the groaning of creation, when we see an animal suffering, or some child, or hear an ambulance pass, we say, "Kyrie eleison!" as the liturgy has taught us. We are priests, remember, through our baptism; and one of the tasks of the priest is to intercede for others who don't or can't pray for themselves.

Gloria

Then the Gloria. *Gloria in excelsis Deo!* On Sundays of the year, except in Advent and Lent, and on many solemn and festive occasions the Gloria is said or sung. The most thrilling of all the times when it is sung occurs during the Great Vigil of Easter, when, after light has been brought into the darkened church, and we have heard the Exsultet, and have moved slowly and inexorably in the readings from the Old Testament through the ages of waiting for our redemption, we hear the priest intone *Gloria!* Light floods the church, the organ peals, bells ring, and we, the faithful, cry out in response, "And peace to his people on earth!" joining our voices with all of heaven and earth in this triumphant hymn of acclamation to God.

The hymn, which goes back to Christian antiquity, presents us with words of pure praise. Praise is not an easy activity for us: left to our own devices we lapse into thanksgiving to God for his blessings (which is certainly a good thing to do, but it is not quite synonymous with praise). We need to turn to texts like the Psalms or the Te Deum or the Gloria to find words that will give shape to the act of praise for us.

The hymn addresses the Father and the Son, speaks of excellences and perfections which belong to each, invokes God's mercy, and concludes with a Trinitarian formula. To someone unfamiliar with praise, this business of merely reiterating the fact that we are praising (the Latin makes the reiteration more vivid: *laudamus te, benedicimus te, adoramus te, glorificamus te, gratias agimus tibi . . .*) might seem somewhat obvious and even gratuitous. Well, then (the observer might object), let's get on with the praising and leave off telling him that we are praising. But as far back as we can reach into history and myth, this phenomenon of *saying* that we are praising, or of calling upon others to do so ("Praise the Lord!") has constituted the very act of praise.

And along with this phenomenon we find another peculiarity of praise, namely, the sheer itemizing for God of his own perfections, which surely he already knows about. What is achieved by our telling him, "For you alone are the Holy One"? The Psalms are full of this sort of thing, as is Christian hymnody.

The answer is that praise, or worship actually, takes us beyond the merely "useful", the utilitarian, we might say, into that realm where the calling back and forth in the great seraphic antiphons of what is *true* turns out to be the central activity of the universe. Or put it this way around: the truth (for example, God is holy) is such that it outstrips mere proposition or "fact", and is rightly apprehended by us creatures, finally, in exultation. It is not neutral or inert, as mere propositions might suggest. Discourse and syllogism can assist us as we creep toward what may be true. But when we find ourselves having burst into the courts of Truth itself, then our propositions die on our tongues and our syllogisms collapse. We must either be silent, awestruck, or we must take up that form of utterance which alone answers to what truth is, namely, song.

Song—hymn, canticle, psalm—is not "useful". It butters no bread. It argues no case, nor explains any riddle. It acclaims. It extols. It lauds. It lauds that which is laudable. And to learn to do this is to be taken out of the sinkhole of egoism into which our sin plunged us at the Fall and to begin to take our true place in the universal chorus, which includes all things, from the seraphim right on down to the north wind, the surf, the mountains and edelweiss and the song of the winter wren and the atoms—that chorus which exults in what is true, and which cries, *"Gloria!"*

Opening Prayer

After the Gloria we come to the Opening Prayer, or Collect. A collect is a prayer which "collects up", so to speak, petitions that are appropriate to the day, and articulates them as a sort of touchstone for the day's liturgy. Like the Entrance Song, it is a sort of tuning fork, setting the pitch for the rest of the liturgy, giving us a concentrated act of supplication and petition to the Lord. If it is Lent, then the Collect makes some request fitting for this time of penitence and reflection. If it is Advent, then the Collect turns our attention to this time of anticipation and preparation. If it is the commemoration of a martyr or a doctor of the Church or some other saint, then that one is mentioned by name. The Collect gathers us into one praying congregation—we at Mass, who are a random clutter of people. It helps give a shape to our thoughts as we move on into the readings from Scripture, which now follow.

6

God's Word Proclaimed

The Bible comes into its own in a particular way
in the liturgy. Certainly it is to be read and pon-
dered day by day by all of the faithful. It is one of
the mainstays of our sustenance. We may recall the
words of the prophet Jeremiah: "Thy words were
found, and I ate them, and thy words became to
me a joy and the delight of my heart" (Jer 15:16).
And the Psalms are full of testimony to the place
the Word of God has in the inner being of the
godly man. "I have laid up thy word in my heart,
that I might not sin against thee" (Ps 119:11). Our
Lord himself was clearly steeped in Scripture from
his earliest youth.

But the Church from the beginning understood that Scripture appears in its most characteristic usage when it is read aloud at the liturgy.
For here the Law and the Prophets and the

Gospels and Epistles and Psalms take their place as essential components of the central activity of the Church, namely, the celebration of the Eucharist. Here the entire drama of our redemption is unfurled day by day, and hence here we encounter the words of Scripture with a particular clarity and force. We begin, in truth, to see the seamlessness of the fabric of redemption rather than encountering the Word as a rather loosely knit quilt, say, of words from on high—God's Word, to be sure, but not always connected to the rest of the pieces. In the fabric of the liturgy and of the liturgical year the pattern begins to emerge.

On Sundays and other feast days there are three readings ordinarily—one from the Old Testament (or the Acts of the Apostles), one from the Epistles (or Revelation), and then one from the Gospel. On most weekdays only two readings are offered, with the second being always the Gospel. After the first reading on all days a "responsorial Psalm" is said, with the reader or cantor reciting the text of a Psalm and the people responding after each brief section with a refrain based on one of the Psalm's own lines (usually). The cycle of readings (of Sunday and weekday liturgies) over three years gives a review of the entire Bible.

"Thanks Be to God"

There are two or three things worth noting in the Liturgy of the Word.

First, the response asked of us, the faithful, would seem to be a small matter—just a detail of the liturgy scarcely worth noting. "Thanks be to God", we say. What could be more routine or innocuous?

But if we will pause a moment to think of what we are saying, we may find the matter somewhat daunting. Thanks be to God? But suppose the reading has brought to our attention some alarming account of God's dealings with his people— Abraham obliged to sacrifice his son Isaac, say, or Moses' wrath when he finds the people capering around the golden calf, or Nathan with his dire "thou art the man" to the sinful King David? These are not soothing narratives. They come at us fiercely and jog us with the picture of God's inscrutable holiness or of his mysterious will. Left to our own spontaneous reactions, we might, if we were candid, incline rather to respond, "Not now, thanks", or "Could we have another, more consoling, text, please?" But, says the liturgy, "Thanks be to God" is *the* response asked of us to the Word of God, no matter how unsettling or inconvenient it may be at the moment.

The matter, apparently so small a detail of the liturgy, brings us right up to one of the central junctures of the whole divine drama, namely, the Annunciation, where this Word of God came to the Virgin, no doubt highly inconveniently, and certainly alarmingly. The message altered her entire life forever. Any local agenda she might have had evaporated at one stroke. But—we hear her say, "Be it done unto me according to thy word."

In her we see the authentic human response to the approach of God. Whereas you and I in our father Adam and our mother Eve said, "Be it done unto me according to *my* (or Satan's!) word", Mary said, "according to thy word". It is this response that is put into our mouths by the liturgy. Hell, or what amounts to the same thing, self-will, loathes and fears God's Word. "Away with him!" cries the rebellious human heart. But we the faithful are to place ourselves day by day among those men and women, Mary first of all, who hear the Word of God and receive it gladly, and configure our lives accordingly.

If we suppose that such difficulties arise only with respect to Old Testament readings, we may recall such Pauline admonitions as "Be kind to one another, tenderhearted, forgiving one another, as God in Christ forgave you" (Eph 4:32). Hmm. There's matter worth pondering. Tenderhearted? But this person with whom I am obliged to live is a slovenly and malicious bore. He needs to be knocked on the head, and if I don't do it, who will? Tenderhearted? That person tries my patience beyond what any reasonable person can be asked to endure. She needs a good tongue-lashing, and I know exactly what to say. Forgiving one another? No. I've had enough of this person's venom and spite. He needs a dose of his own medicine now, and I have just the prescription, all mixed and ready.

Alas. Such hellish turbulence tosses to and fro in our thoughts. And here is the Epistle not only telling me to be tenderhearted and forgiving (or telling me that the fruit of the Spirit is peace and long-suffering and gentleness and *meekness*, forsooth), but obliging me to answer, "Thanks be to God."

The liturgy is a strong and faithful tutor. If we will pay attention to it and dispose ourselves to assent and desire to come, albeit slowly, into those precincts of felicity to which the liturgy bids us, then indeed we will find ourselves "assisting at" the celebration more and more wholeheartedly.

Responsorial Psalm

The Responsorial Psalm, which comes after the first reading, might seem to be a sort of pause in things. And in one sense it is. Here is ancient Hebrew poetry, so beautiful, so full of the deepest aspirations of the human heart. "Like as a hart . . ." or, "Out of the depths . . ." Can we not just sit back and luxuriate in the beauty of these lines?

Well, yes and no. Yes, if by that we mean that it is a good and pleasant thing to attune one's ears to that which is both beautiful and true, or, to employ a more extravagant metaphor, to let the tide of psalmody wash around our fevered souls. Yes. But no, if by that we imply that what we have in psalmody is a sort of aesthetic interlude. No. The Psalms are the songs of Zion; that is, they are the most profound utterance of the human heart as it makes its way through this world to the Mount of God. In them we encounter the human person in all of its mystery as it struggles to articulate itself *in conspectu Dei* (in the sight of God). Every one of man's deepest experiences and thoughts—grief, rage, relief, hilarity, doubt, despondency, perplexity, acedia, triumph—they are all here. But they are all here *referred to God*. The psalmist's very fury or doubt is spread out before the Most High. We might say that this is the poetry of the human heart as it opens itself to God (as opposed, say, to the tedium which we find in the self-absorption of a Whitman). No human emotion, thought, or experience is huddled out of sight in the Psalms. All is spread out *in conspectu Dei*.

And that, certainly, is the frame of mind which we the faithful gathered at the liturgy wish to attain. What is life like, lived *in conspectu Dei*? We have a human testimony to this in Augustine's *Confessions*: the entire autobiography, literally every paragraph of it, is addressed directly "to thee, O Lord". In the Psalms we have this record, but raised to the dignity of God's Word. (We all have great difficulty with the imprecatory Psalms: How can that cursing be God's Word? Of course it isn't, if we mean that it is God's Word to us as to how to handle our rage. But there it is included in the canon of Scripture, a salutary reminder that "the wrath of God" is a fully biblical idea.)

In the special form in which the liturgy presents the Psalms to us we find yet another cue, so to speak, about how things are in the court of heaven. It is the quality of antiphonality. For the Responsorial Psalm, the reader reads a few lines, and then we all answer with a recurring refrain.

More than a dozen times in the Mass we are called upon to respond to something that has been said, to answer a greeting: "And also with you", "We lift them up to the Lord", or "Amen." This calling back and forth is, as we have already noted in the Gloria, one of the properties of heaven or, shall we say, of joy. That is, we all know the satisfaction which comes when we find that we are in glad agreement with what someone is saying. Yes! Exactly! I couldn't agree more! You've said it better than I could have! And this satisfaction soars to great heights when we find ourselves in a company—or better, a throng—who all agree. Such camaraderie! Such glorious affirmation! *Ecce quam bonum* . . . (Ps 133)!

This is a hint of the joy of heaven. We have fugitive glimpses of this in Saint John's Apocalypse, where we hear voices calling back and forth. And Hebrew poetry is set up so that the lines themselves "call back and forth" to each other ("Let the sea roar . . . let the floods clap their hands" [Ps 98:7, 8], or "Praise him with sounding cymbals . . . praise him with loud clashing cymbals" [Ps 150:5])—antiphonality.

It must have something to do with the very structure of reality. It seems meet and right that things be uttered, sent forth, received by assenting voices, and returned, affirmed. Reality is not inert. It is structured so that it reverberates with the truth. It echoes the truth. It exults in the truth. The universe, all creatures and things, all angels and saints, invite us, "Come, join the Dance." The antiphons of the Mass are early training in *the* great choreography, in *the* great ringing antiphon before the eternal *perichoresis*, the "Dance" of the Persons of the Trinity.

The seraphim know this; and in the liturgy we begin to be introduced into this blissful antiphonality. When we respond to the Psalm, we are taking our first steps in the Dance.

Gospel

Anyone who assists at the liturgy regularly will observe that the reading of the Gospel is set about with great solemnity. On feast days (and in the old High Mass) the Gospel book is taken from the altar, the reader is blessed, and a procession with lights and incense brings the book to the lectern, where the reading takes place. But even if we find ourselves at an ordinary weekday Mass with only three or four people present, we find that the reading of the Gospel is preceded by a "Gospel acclamation" (an introductory text from Scripture) and by the singing of Alleluia. The congregation stands: a sign of our readiness, of our anticipation of Christ's return in glory. Then, as the priest or deacon says, "A reading from the holy Gospel according to Luke" (say), he and we make a small threefold sign of the Cross on forehead, lips, and breast. Clearly we are approaching a most holy moment here, and it is essential that our entire being, our thoughts, words, and affections, be found under the Cross of Jesus Christ, which is the sign of perfect obedience to the Father's will.

For the Gospel is, in a unique way, God himself speaking to his people from the midst of that people. That is, when he came to us in the Incarnation, he was "Immanuel", God with us. And the words which we heard him speak by Galilee, on the mountain, and in Jerusalem and Capernaum were God's words being spoken to his people from among them.

And once more we respond, this time with "Praise to you, Lord Jesus Christ." In some ways this may be more daunting than the mere "Thanks be to God" asked of us in the other readings, since the Gospel takes the rigorous injunctions of the Old Testament Law (say, "Thou shalt not kill") and carries them right into the inner man, warning us that *anger*, forsooth, at another person is tantamount to murder.

This is very dismaying on the surface of it. It is one thing to refrain from getting a pistol and shooting someone; but how on earth am I to keep rage from my heart?

You cannot on earth, would be the appropriate reply. But the life into which we have been born at our baptism and which the Holy Spirit ministers to us in the Scriptures and in the sacraments is a divine life; and in that life not only is there no murder committed: anger itself, and vituperation, and sullenness, and resentment, and vengefulness are all expunged. And it is this divine life that is beginning to grow and to bud and flower and bear fruit in us. It does not happen all in the twinkling of an eye. The saints themselves tell us of the rigors entailed in the school of charity.

But we are en route. And one of the things that will help us is our being obliged to receive the saving Gospel with "Praise to you, Lord Jesus Christ" (you, who are our Savior, and who will bring us to that realm where we have won through to the unimaginable freedom that crowns the men and women who have received the Gospel with joy).

Homily

After the Gospel comes the homily. This is the point in the liturgy when the faithful are given instruction or admonition or solace or encouragement from the deacon, priest, or bishop, drawn directly from the preceding readings, most especially the Gospel. Saint Paul lays great stress on the importance of teaching in the Church. In the Protestant tradition, with the disappearance of the sacraments from the center of focus, the preaching of the Word took on that central place, and sermons (homilies) became the main point in going to church. Such sermons depend more and more on the ingenuity and resourcefulness of the preacher himself; and in some denominations there is encouraged a highly elaborate art of constructing sermons, complete with alliteration or other rhetorical devices, that adds up, finally, to an Oration, very often forty-five minutes long.

This has not been the path followed by the Catholic Church. Ordinarily the homily is fairly brief (often ten minutes or even less). And the emphasis is placed on linking the various readings and pointing out to the faithful some common theme culminating in the Gospel text for the day.

Yet the homily is not a diversion in our active worship, a parenthesis blurring our focus. Instruction in the Word is part of the seamless fabric of our act as Church when we come to offer the sacrifice of praise. We place ourselves under the scrutiny and teaching of Scripture.

It must be said that the homily, from time to time in the Church's history, finds itself in low water. We ourselves may be in just such an epoch now. In some cases homilies are perfunctory or hastily assembled or platitudinous, or even nonexistent (announcements fill up the time slot). This was not the apostolic idea for the homily. We all have a model in the person of Pope John Paul II of homiletics as it can (and should) be. His homilies are intensely Bible centered, and they probe to the marrow of the texts in question. There never fails to be a profound challenge to the faithful—a challenge to obedience, to holiness, and to courage and increased ardor in these homilies.

For our part we, the faithful, should have in our minds the words of our Lord when the woman in the crowd rhapsodized on the womb that bore him and the breasts which suckled him: "Blessed rather are those who hear the word of God and keep it" (Lk 11:28) is his response to zeal like this. It is a good rubric for us as we listen to the homily.

7

Profession of Faith and Intercessions

Creed

The Creed follows the homily. It might seem at first glance an odd ingredient in the liturgy, this rote recitation of the bald data about God, and about Jesus Christ, and the Holy Spirit, and several matters attached to the end. Isn't this sort of thing more appropriate to a catechism class?

It is indeed appropriate to catechesis; but the Church knew what she was doing when, early on, she introduced into the rites and ceremonies for the faithful when they gathered this corporate and vocal affirmation of the faith. Here we have not merely a repeating of a formula, like the multiplication table, that everyone ought to know by heart; it is that, to be sure. But appearing as it does in the liturgy, it takes on a *solemnity*. That is, it takes on a certain weight and dignity, and there is even a note of exultation here which accords well with the whole action of the liturgy. We Christians believe in—in what God? Ahura Mazda? Phtha? Moloch? Jove? These are all the gods of the nations, as the Psalms put the matter. But we—we believe in one God, the Father, the Almighty, maker of heaven and earth. And in his Son. And in the Holy Spirit. And in one, holy, catholic, and apostolic Church. And in the forgiveness of sins, and so forth and so forth. There, like a great banner unfurled for all heaven, earth, and hell to see, is what we—Christians—believe. Even as we repeat it we find that its glorious phrases (". . . eternally begotten of the Father . . . he came down from heaven . . . he rose again . . .") take on the character of joy. We not only *repeat* this; we seem to find ourselves saying: we laud, we extol, we adore, we exult in these immensities.

The Creed is a point of particular dignity in the liturgy.

General Intercessions

The general intercessions, or prayer of the faithful, follows the Creed. With a brief opening phrase or sentence, we are bidden to bring our intentions (requests) to God. Or rather, it is not so much our personal intentions as those of the Church herself. Ideally we enter into these intentions and make them our own. The usual format is for the priest, the deacon, or a lay person to announce each intention. The congregation responds to each with "Lord, hear our prayer" or a similar response.

This part of the liturgy ushers us into one of the most profound mysteries of the Christian faith. It is the mystery that attends all prayer to begin with, and which no doubt every one of us has puzzled over at some point, namely, that prayer exists at all: How can *our* petitions alter the titanic march of events? There is, of course, no satisfactory answer to the question if it is posed like that. No picture or equation will throw much light on the "connection" between what appear to us to be two irreconcilables, namely, happenstance (or chance—the way things just seem to occur with no discernible rhyme or reason) and the will of God. Every effort we put forth to unravel the skein frustrates us. If chance is what it seems to be, then God is not running things. Or, if he is running things, then he seems to be a capricious deity. To believe as the Church does that he is both all-powerful and also all-loving obliges us to relinquish our equations and to enter the darkness in faith. Even the book of Job gives us no "answer" other than "Where were you when I made the snow?" (cf. Job 39), and so forth. Even Saint Paul demurs with "Can the clay demand reasons from the potter?" (cf. Rom 9:20).

The intercessions bring us close to these impenetrable questions, since we are asking the Most High to do this and that which would seem to cut across or alter the immense unrolling of sheer events. For example, we pray for peace in the world, and yet we all know that wars and rumors of wars will go on until the end (our Lord himself told us so). And do we suppose that such prayers will suddenly bring tranquil solutions to ravaged areas like (as of this writing) Bosnia, Rwanda, or the Middle East? Or again, we pray for the sick. What, exactly (someone might urge), do we have in mind? That they will get well? Now? Do we suppose the hospitals will empty out because we have prayed? If not, then what is it we are asking? That they will be comforted and encouraged? Do we imagine that sickbeds across the world will each be touched with some warm breath bringing solace, if only momentarily?

To press such questions is to reduce the mystery of prayer to frivolity; and yet an interlocutor might want to know what, then, we *do* hope for from the Church's intercessions.

The Church's response would run something like this: in prayer, and most eloquently in the corporate prayer of the faithful gathered in the liturgy, we see the Body, of which Jesus Christ is the Head, drawn into the mystery of his priestly self-offering for the life of the world. He offered up his life on the altar of Calvary to his Father on behalf of suffering, sinful mankind. Somehow all suffering and all sin was subsumed in that perfect offering of his. Healing for ten thousand times the suffering of our world pours forth from Calvary with his Blood; and forgiveness in a superabundance that dwarfs our tally of sin.

That offering went up to the Father and was received. But Jerusalem was not aware of it the next morning. The lepers still crouched at the roadside in their rags, and widows still mourned their dead, and urchins still scavenged for some crumb of offal to fill their stomachs. By any of a thousand tests the thing had been futile.

But no, says faith. No, says the Church. We do not yet see the fruit of that redemption wrought for us by the Son of God at Calvary. We live in hope. We strain toward the Day when it will be revealed. The very creation groans and travails, says Saint Paul, awaiting the deliverance that has been promised—nay, that has been achieved.

But so far we grasp this fruition in faith, as hope.

And meanwhile, we, the Church, far from sitting idly awaiting the Day when God will wipe away all tears, find that in a mystery we are drawn in to this very self-offering of our Head. We offer ourselves and our intercessions for the life of the world. We have not been made privy to the councils of the Most High where the irreconcilables are knit together. We see the same havoc and ruin and agony as do those who, in the name of suffering, fling blasphemies in the face of God who, they say, either cannot or will not help. We cannot offer them the equation that will allay their fury. We share the same flesh and blood as they. And there may be many times in the presence of human suffering and evil when we are obliged to bow our heads and say, "Yes, I know", rather than bustling in with "But the answer is . . ." Our silence, though, should pulsate with an interior "Kyrie eleison! Jesus, Savior, help!"

We are brought to such a point in the liturgy at the intercessions. We take our place, as it were, with Jesus Christ the Savior, our Head, who, in his self-offering, found that the sky was shrouded with black clouds. No ray came from heaven, where multitudes of angels stood ready to ride out and scatter the evil that had brought things to this pass. On that day the offering up was all. The answer was not yet apparent—and is still not apparent in its fullness two thousand years later. The world still suffers, and the Church still offers up prayer. Our place is at the altar, Calvary, where offering is made. We have not been invited to the bench where judgment is given.

But of course in the day-to-day experience of the liturgy we do not find that the darkness of these huge riddles suddenly descends on us. We seldom are granted the clarity which pierces through the scrim of ordinariness into the darkness. Most of the time we simply "get on with it". We join in the intercessions. And this is as it should be. We are mortal (it is a salutary thing to recall), and as T. S. Eliot, in *Four Quartets*, expressed it, "Human kind cannot bear very much reality." Our mortal frame cannot shoulder the burden of the universe.

This consideration points us to one of the richest aspects of the liturgy. The liturgy is at one and the same time a daily discipline as "do-able" as walking to the corner or eating our lunch, and the entry into the highest mysteries of heaven. We all know this, if we reflect for a moment; but it is a mark of the liturgy's extraordinary genius that in the restraint and sobriety of its ritual (words) and ceremony it mediates inexhaustible and ineffable mysteries to us in terms that meet our ordinariness, and that neither stun us nor wear thin over the centuries.

8

Preparation of the Gifts

At this point the Liturgy of the Eucharist proper
begins with the preparation of the altar and the
gifts. So far there have occurred the introductory
rites and the Liturgy of the Word. This was called
the *synaxis* (gathering) in the early Church. We
now come to the *anaphora* (offering).

The priest takes the paten (on which rests the
wafer) and, holding it slightly raised, blesses God
for his goodness in supplying us with bread; this
bread will become for us the bread of life, says the
prayer.

In so brief an act we find ourselves yet again
hailed with immense mysteries. This bread will
become for us the bread of life? How so? All bread
is the bread of life, surely: the whole world acknowledges bread as the staff of life. Is the liturgy
dilating on the obvious here?

Yes and no (as is so often the case in the liturgy). Yes, in the sense that we do indeed bless God, as we ought to do always, for his munificence in sending rain and sunshine, age after age, on the earth so that crops will grow and we will eat. It is most fitting to bless God thus.

But no, in the sense that these words carry us infinitely beyond the obvious. The liturgy, says the Church, is the sacramental act par excellence in which utterly ordinary things (bread, in this case) are taken and, being offered to God with a particular intention, are received by him, changed, and given to us as the very Bread of Heaven. In this brief blessing the liturgy anticipates the central mystery of the Mass that will occur presently, namely, the fulfillment of the Lord's promise that he would give us his Flesh to eat and his Blood to drink.

And as is always the case, we find that what is enacted here in the liturgy illumines the whole fabric of life for us. That is, here we bring ordinary things (bread); and God, receiving them in his mercy, returns them to us transfigured—transubstantiated, really: the very substance has become divine. By the same token, Christians find that, insofar as the "prayers, works, joys, and sufferings of this day" (the ordinary stuff of life) are taken and offered up to God in union with Jesus Christ's own self-offering, they are transfigured—transubstantiated—and restored to us, not as the inert routines of the day, or as sheer, intractable adversity, or as boredom, which they might otherwise appear to be, but rather as vessels for grace.

For example, I may find myself, if I live outside of a great city, obliged to cope every morning with deadly traffic jams. The minutes tick away maddeningly, and here I sit on this expressway (the very name a mockery). What a waste. But there is no way around it. It is nettlesome in the extreme.

But the Church teaches us that if we take this very thing—this intractable ordinariness, this frustration—and "offer it up", we will find that the very thing itself becomes the occasion for blessing. It may be that I not only need to learn patience (but what a vexing method of teaching you have, Lord!) but also to know God in a way I could not otherwise enter into. The implacable hand of daily circumstance becomes, lo, the hand of the Divine Mercy itself.

That is a relatively superficial case in point of the thing. The Church teaches, in the light of Scripture ("I complete what is lacking in Christ's afflictions", says Saint Paul [Col 1:24]; and "I have been crucified with Christ" [Gal 2:20]) that our suffering may, in a mystery, be offered to God in union with Christ's oblation at Calvary, and that as such this suffering is transfigured—transubstanti-ated, even—so that it is given back to us from the Divine Mercy itself, not now as sheer, mere, grim horror, but rather as the occasion for grace—grace in me the sufferer and grace for those who see it at work in me.

One hesitates even to sketch out a scenario like this. How will I do when my turn comes? Very little has been asked of me so far. And how can I speak so blithely about *suffering* in the face of uni-versal pain that rebuffs my cavalier exordium?

One cannot, on one's own. One is in no posi-tion at all to speak. But the liturgy brings us to this frontier where all of us, fortunate and unfortunate, may encounter the mystery whereby God's grace takes what we bring to him—*anything*—and changes its substance, by the same mystery which turned the Crucifixion, that most botched of all miserable events, into the salvation of the world. This which I find to be my lot (this obscurity or weariness, or this twisted spine or malignant tu-mor, or this daunting task, or even the unobtrusive routines of my day)—*this* may be brought as the bread is brought at the preparation of the gifts to be changed by grace into salvation for me.

But most of us will want to speak here only hesitantly, if at all: it is to be left to those who know what long-suffering is to speak with much warrant.

In some celebrations of the Mass, we may see the bread and wine being brought in vessels from the back of the church to the priest at the altar. This rite is an enacting of what we have been speaking of here, as though to say, "Here we come, Lord, with our daily quota of ordinariness or of extraordinary suffering: do thou take it, and receive it, and make it the very substance of salvation for us."

Our response to the words of blessing that the priest says over the bread is "Blessed be God for ever." Again, a mouthful. We praise him both for his bounty in creation and in supplying our needs, but also for the mystery of his grace, so painful to us as it may be at times, whereby he transforms the stuff of our life into glory.

The priest then mingles a drop or two of water with the wine in the chalice. It is a sign of the uniting in Jesus Christ of our humanity with his deity, *and also* of the great mystery of grace whereby we mortals are raised to share in the life of God himself. The Orthodox Church speaks of the "deification" of man, by which it does not

mean that we slough off our humanity and become gods, but rather that the fruition of the entire drama of redemption is that we mortals come
to share the life of the Holy Trinity. This is what
the Church teaches; and we have a momentary
glimpse of this immense fruition just here in the
words the priest says as he pours wine and water
into the chalice.

Then, as he blessed God for the bread, so he
blesses God for his gift of the vine, from which we
men have made wine. And again we respond,
"Blessed be God for ever." (This is not a bad phrase
for us to have on our tongues repeatedly during
the day. Sooner or later we will have to learn to say
it wholeheartedly, since it is the language of
heaven. Hell, on the other hand, has only irrita-
tion and curses on its tongue.)

After this preparation of the bread and wine,
the priest bows and asks, on behalf of us all, that
God will be pleased with the sacrifice we are about
to offer. The sacrifice is, on one level, the offering
of ourselves, our petitions, and our worship—that
is, the entire liturgy. But on a deeper level, what is
referred to is Jesus Christ's own sacrifice of himself
at Calvary in our behalf.

Two things may be kept in mind at this point.
First, many people both inside and outside the

Catholic Church suppose that in the Mass Catholics believe that Jesus is sacrificed again and again and again, innumerable times down through the centuries. This is a confusion arising no doubt from a failure to grasp what the Church actually believes in this connection. The Mass is, as we have already seen, an *anamnesis*—a recalling which is also a making present. Jesus Christ died two thousand years ago. But he is, we may remember from Scripture (Rev 13:8), "the Lamb slain from the foundation of the world". The Church believes that Jesus Christ's self-offering took place, to be sure, at a real point in history and not in a myth (this is why we say "he was crucified under Pontius Pilate" in the Creed: we are talking about real, light-of-day human history here). But at the same time, in a mystery, this sacrifice at Calvary is eternally present in the heavenly realities, and the liturgy takes us through the scrim that hangs between time and eternity into that realm where we find the one Priest (Jesus Christ), the one Sacrifice (Jesus himself), and the one Altar (the Cross). It is this sacrifice and no other, nor any mere repetition, that is made present in the liturgy, says the Church. Hence, when Catholics speak of the Mass as a "sacrifice", they mean neither some sacrifice *other than* the Cross, nor do they mean some numerical repeating of the one Sacrifice at the Cross. The Eucharist is a sacrament (a "mystery"), not a mechanical repeating of something.

Second, the Church teaches that any sacrifice or offering which we make to God is accepted by him in virtue of Jesus Christ's sacrifice of himself in our behalf. We are not worthy ourselves to enter the precincts of the heavenly throne; nor do we possess anything that is not already God's (after all, he made us and everything in our world) and which qualifies, so to speak, by itself as a worthy offering. But insofar as we unite ourselves with Jesus Christ in his offering we find that we and all that we offer are received. Here is how the *Catechism of the Catholic Church* speaks of this matter:

> The Eucharist is the memorial of Christ's Passover, the making present and the sacramental offering of his unique sacrifice, in the liturgy of the Church which is his Body . . . (1362). When the Church celebrates the Eucharist, she commemorates Christ's Passover, and it is made present: the sacrifice Christ offered once for all on the cross remains ever present . . . (1364; cf. Heb 7:25–27). The sacrifice of Christ and the sacrifice of the Eucharist are *one single sacrifice* . . . (1367). The Church which is the Body of Christ

participates in the offering of her Head. With him, she herself is offered whole and entire. She unites herself to his intercession with the Father for all men. In the Eucharist the sacrifice of Christ becomes also the sacrifice of the members of his Body. The lives of the faithful, their praise, sufferings, prayer, and work, are united with those of Christ and with his total offering . . . (1368).

All of this is bespoken when the priest says, "Be pleased with the sacrifice we offer you."

Then we see the priest ritually wash his hands. "Lord, wash away my iniquity; cleanse me from my sin." We may recall the familiar Psalm here: "Who shall ascend the hill of the LORD? And who shall stand in his holy place? He who has clean hands and a pure heart" (Ps 24:3–4). Any priest entering the place of sacrifice in the Old Testament had to be cleansed. But we the congregation are also, by virtue of our baptism, "priests" (see *Catechism*, 1546, 1547), and since we are about to participate in holy things, we may take this moment to make that prayer our own.

Then, turning to us, the priest asks us to pray that our sacrifice may be acceptable to God, and we respond, "May the Lord accept the sacrifice at your hands for the praise and glory of his name, for our good, and the good of all his Church." This response on our part focuses our attention on the *point* of what we are about to do: it is an act of worship ("for the praise and glory of his name"); and it is an act that benefits us ("for our good") and the whole Church, since it is the sacrifice of Jesus Christ that is the fountainhead of every blessing for us. And in what we are about to do we find ourselves at the Lord's Table itself, where we are fed with the Food which alone can give us eternal life.

9

Eucharistic Prayer

Preface

After a brief prayer over the gifts (for example, "Lord, be pleased with the gifts we bring to your altar, and make them the sacrament of our salvation" [Fourth Sunday in Ordinary Time]), the priest says, "The Lord be with you", and we respond, "And also with you." A routine greeting. Merely a liturgical convention. Yes, but like every phrase and gesture in the Mass, these words are themselves filled with meaning. For in this unobtrusive exchange between priest and people, we hear the language of heaven, really. It is in that realm where Charity presides that we hear greetings like this: every being calling out to every other being, "May all joy and goodness and glory be your portion! May the Lord himself be with you!" And once more we hear antiphonality: deep calling to deep, as it does all across the fabric of the universe, but most excellently in the City of God. "And also with you!" This is what Charity always has on its lips for everyone it meets; and the liturgy is our tutor here. It puts in our mouths the right words: as we learn to say them, the habit may seep into our inner being. Hell, or egoism, of course, hates this sort of greeting. "Out of my way, fool", says hell. "Am I my brother's keeper?" says the sullen Cain. Alas—an attitude all too recognizable to me, since I know my own heart. May these words, ritually spoken, become the greeting of my heart to all other selves.

Then, "Lift up your hearts." *Sursum corda*. And yet again the immediate detail in the liturgy—just a phrase here—reaches to the most profound depths of the human mystery. We were made to do this. The great dignity that crowned Adam and Eve, and which is the hallmark of our humanity, as distinguished from all the beauties and perfections exhibited by the animals—grace, speed, quickness, suppleness—this dignity consists in our having been made uniquely in the image of God; and the activity proper to that image is this lifting up of the heart to him. It is a gesture that gathers up everything we are and do. In it we not only acknowledge that we live *in conspectu Dei*; we also freely exercise the noble duty and privilege that is ours uniquely, of raising our hearts to him, that is, of saying in effect, "We are thine, O Lord; thou art our Maker, our King, our Savior, and our highest Good. All that we are belongs to thee. We freely raise our hearts to thee in adoration, exultation, thanksgiving, and obedience."

The words that the liturgy puts into our mouths are never idle words. And it is as though the liturgy, aware of the great weight attaching to such words, gives us a moment to ponder them: we approach the act of lifting our hearts by means of the priest's bidding, and *then* we respond, "We lift them up to the Lord." Once again antiphonality draws us into the solemn, measured, rhythmic movement proper to matters of such weight.

A second exchange, "Let us give thanks . . . It is right . . ." brings us to the Preface. The words which we hear the priest now saying bring us, in the light of the feast or season that obtains on this day (Advent, Lent, the Ascension), to the great hymn which Isaiah heard the seraphim crying when he was granted a glimpse of the heavenly court. "Holy, holy, holy." It is an acclamation of nearly insupportable solemnity. We mortals scarcely know how to dispose ourselves properly for a moment like this. The Preface helps us. Acknowledging that to bring just such an acclamation to the Most High is to do well (the Latin is wonderful here: *Vere dignum et justum est . . .*), the Preface then focuses on one aspect of God's saving actions toward us and, in the light of such acts, links our mortal praises with that of "all the choirs of angels" as they cry Holy!

In this great hymn we come upon the word *Hosanna*. Not a word often encountered. It is the Greek form of the Hebrew petition "Save, we beseech thee", which the crowd in Jerusalem cried in greeting to the Lord as he entered the city on a donkey. And we find ourselves calling out their greeting: "Blessed is he who comes in the name of the Lord." The crowd in Jerusalem were no doubt confused and swept away with ill-defined enthusiasm. They had only the dimmest notions of what they were saying. But we, in the liturgy, do know: we greet him who comes to us now on this altar, in this solemnity, under the humble species of bread and wine, as he came humbly long ago on a donkey. He has this way of coming to us inauspiciously and unobtrusively.

Canon of the Mass

The liturgy now approaches its apex. The congregation (in most places) kneels. The great Eucharistic Prayer, or Canon, is about to begin.

The whole liturgy may be seen as one single prayer in one sense, since it is primarily addressed to God, and all of its parts, even those which technically are addressed to us, such as the readings from Scripture or the homily—all of its parts taken together constitute the Church's joyful and obedient response to the invitation from the Divine Mercy to "come and dine". All is "offering" here—all prayers, all acclamations, all ritual and ceremonial actions, and the whole goes up to the Throne like the smoke of incense.

The whole liturgy, then, is the prayer of the Church; but here in the Canon of the Mass we come to the culmination of all that has preceded this point.

What we hear the priest saying at the altar is a form of words that has come down to us from the beginning. The earliest records we have of what actually occurred when the Church gathered for worship with the apostles and, after they died, with the bishops appointed by them, give us the principal elements of this prayer. As the years passed, the liturgy developed and was greatly enriched: but it was an organic development, and the original "backbone" is still clearly there.

The Church offers us nowadays four principal forms for this prayer (along with several others for special uses). At any given celebration of the Mass we will hear, ordinarily, one of these basic four. The pattern of each one begins with a direct address to God the Father. Mention is made of who God is and of what he has done, most especially in creation and in redemption. The "gifts" (that is, the bread and the wine) are presented with the supplication that he will receive them. The First Eucharistic Prayer, or Roman Canon—which had been the only Canon in use in the Latin Rite for more than 1,600 years—offers a long commemoration of the Blessed Virgin, Joseph, the apostles, martyrs, and other saints: we the faithful being thus reminded of the real, literal company among whom we find ourselves as we pray; it is not solely we who are visible in the immediate gathering in this place; the whole Church, because of the victory which the Savior won over death, is knit into one living body—we here, and those who pray with us all over the globe, and those who have died. The Fourth Eucharistic Prayer "reviews" the Gospel: when man fell into sin, "you did not abandon him to the power of death . . . in the fullness of time you sent your only Son to be our Savior." We are taken through the drama of salvation to the Upper Room.

Consecration

Then, in every case, the scene of the Last Supper is recalled, and the words our Lord himself used as he broke the bread and blessed the cup and distributed them to his disciples are repeated: "This is my body which will be given up for you. . . . This is the cup of my blood, the blood of the new and everlasting covenant. It will be shed for you and for all." Christ says to us, "This is the culmination of the mystery of salvation. I am going to give my Body and Blood to you." No other religion has come even near this notion of God himself actually dying for his people and giving himself to them as their nourishment.

At this point we, who from the very first moment of the Mass have entered into the realm where our Great High Priest ceaselessly offers his own Sacrifice in our behalf, find ourselves hailed with the mystery of mysteries, if we may speak thus, when all in these precincts is a mystery. The Church from the beginning has taken our Lord's words in John 6 at their full import. The bread with which he feeds us is his Body, and the drink he supplies is his Blood. No man has a warrant to leech out the meaning here in the interest of plausibility. Saint Paul asks, "The cup of blessing which we bless, is it not a communion in the blood of Christ? The bread which we break, is it not a communion in the body of Christ?" (1 Cor 10:16). The Church would see the denial of the plain force of these words as a failure of faith amounting virtually to sacrilege (making light of holy things).

We may learn how solemnly the apostolic Church received this dominical and apostolic teaching by listening to old Ignatius, bishop in Antioch, and himself a disciple of John. "Mark ye those who hold strange doctrines touching the grace of Jesus which came to us, how they are contrary to the mind of God. . . . They abstain from eucharist and prayer, because they allow not that the eucharist is the flesh of our Savior Jesus Christ, which flesh suffered for our sins" (*Epistle to the Smyrnaeans*, 6, 2).

And Justin, the great teacher and martyr of the second century, says this: "We do not receive these as common bread or common drink. But just as our Savior Jesus Christ was made flesh through the Word of God and had both flesh and blood for our salvation, so also we have been taught that the food which has been eucharized by the word of prayer from Him is the flesh and blood of the Incarnate Jesus" (*First Apology*, 66, 2).

The unanimous testimony of all the early Fathers is the same on this point. Non-Catholics sometimes suspect that the Catholic Church made up this notion of the miraculous Body and Blood during the Middle Ages, and that it represents an elaboration of, and even a departure from, what the ancient Church believed. Not so. It was Jesus Christ himself who disclosed the mystery to us, Saint Paul who taught it, and the whole Church which received it.

If there is one point above all others at which not only our intellects, but also our very imaginations, halt, it would be at this point in the Mass. Once again, all is mystery in the liturgy: but our imaginations have a way of "visualizing" things—dazzling light, say, when the Trinity is spoken of, or immense and radiant remoteness when heaven is mentioned, or a particular mental picture when the Blessed Mother is invoked. But no pictures help us at all at this point when we are asked to receive, in faith, this mystery that the wafer and the wine become the Body and Blood of the Savior.

Saint Thomas Aquinas acknowledges this in his great hymn on the mystery:

> Therefore we, before him bending,
> This great Sacrament revere;

Types and shadows have their ending,
For the newer rite is here;
Faith, our outward sense befriending,
Makes our inward vision clear.
(*Tantum Ergo*)

As we hear the words of the Consecration we find ourselves in the midst of that immense throng which no man can number, out of every kindred and tribe and people and tongue, none of whom were able to encompass the mystery, but all of whom consented to be found at this Table in obedient and humble response to the bidding of the Savior himself to "take and eat".

In so doing we take up our identity, incomprehensible to the mind of the world, as people who are nourished by *this* Food. What food? A Body pierced and slain; Blood spilled. That speaks of death. But this Food nourishes us with eternal life, that is, with the life of the Holy and Undivided Trinity. How can this be? The "answer" (if we may bring such a word into play in this region of impenetrable mystery) lies somewhere near the paradox that this trinitarian life, this life of God, is, in its very essence (again, if we may speak thus daringly) *poured-out life*. The "exchanges" among the three Persons of the Trinity are of the nature of "self-donation". All that is received is forthwith given. Language staggers here. This hints at the bliss known by God in his trinitarian life and also at how this giving took shape on the stage of our own history, when God came to us in the flesh. He "emptied" himself, and took on him the form of a servant, and became obedient unto death (cf. Phil 2). Death was the final shape which this self-donation took when God gave himself for us. His flesh was the pledge of his total solidarity with us. If we, for our part, wish to enter into the mystery of this divine life—of this self-donation—then we must go the way he went. Self-donation: there is no other way. This is the identity which we claim as we venture to this Table, God help us all. It is holy food spread before us. Saint Paul warns us solemnly against approaching these precincts frivolously or stained with unacknowledged sin. "Let a man examine himself", the Apostle adjures (1 Cor 11:28).

And, upon reflection, we discover that the whole mystery present to us in the Mass—the mystery of God, and of God coming to us, and of his undergoing, in his flesh, death in our behalf, and of his rising, and interceding for us, and, O Magnum Mysterium, of his offering us this Flesh to eat and Blood to drink so that we may have life in us (cf. John 6 again)—we discover that the word to be applied to this entire drama is Love.

Ah. *Domine Deus. Miserere nobis.* How shall we, distracted and wayward and self-absorbed creatures that we are, be changed into the image of this One who is Love incarnate? We bring nothing but a tissue of venality and cravenness and pusillanimity and perfidiousness and vanity. Alas! Lord, I am not worthy! Depart from me, Lord: I am a sinful man! Woe is me! Against thee and thee only have I sinned! Kyrie eleison!

Yes. Just the words for the lips of such as I. Zacchaeus and Peter and Isaiah and David did not think these cries beneath them when they saw the Lord. It is august company amongst which I find myself if I will make these supplications my own.

And what do I hear from the Most High, before whom I bow under the weight of my own frailty and shame? "Neither do I condemn thee. . . . For God sent not his Son into the world to condemn the world, but that the world through him might be saved. . . . Come unto me. . . . Thy sins are forgiven. . . . Come and see. . . . Come and dine."

He brought me into the banqueting house, and his banner over me was love. The words from the Canticle of Canticles supply us with the refrain we need here.

Memorial Acclamation

Then we hear, "Let us proclaim the mystery of faith", and we respond with one of several acclamations which state, in stark and utterly brief form, just what it is which we celebrate here in the liturgy. None of the responses in English corresponds well with the preferred response in the Latin Typical Edition: *Mortem tuam annuntiamus, Domine, et tuam resurrectionem confitemur, donec venias* [We proclaim your death, O Lord, and we confess your resurrection until you come]. "Christ has died, Christ is risen, Christ will come again" is perhaps the most widely used of these acclamations. It is as though the Church summons all of heaven, earth, and hell (yes, the devils) to note. This, and nothing less or other than this, is what we celebrate, O all ye whom we summon to record: we declare, loudly, gladly, and unabashedly, what is *true*! "Dying you destroyed our death, rising you restored our life. Lord Jesus, come in glory", or "When we eat this bread and drink this cup, we proclaim your death, Lord Jesus, until you come in glory", or "Lord, by your Cross and Resurrection you have set us free. You are the Savior of the world." Hear how we address our Savior! rings out in the words.

Perhaps the most astonishing thing about this response which the priest bids from us here is its compactness. Titanic splendors—the wisdom hidden in God for countless ages and unfurled in Judea and Galilee two thousand years ago—are bespoken here. If any Catholic, by the way, is ever called to speak up and say what it is that Catholics believe, he can do no better than to answer with one of these formulas. His interlocutor may be some zealot from a sector of Christendom other than the Catholic Church, or some unbeliever, or even the tempter whispering confusion and doubt in his ear. Well—Christ has died! Christ is (hurray for that present tense of the verb!) risen! Christ will come again! It is a glorious red-and-gold ensign fluttering in the van of this blood-bought multitude among whom we wish to be found. Is this too triumphalistic? In our own time we, perhaps rightly, wish to be known, especially by the world, as servants. The icon of the Lord kneeling, girt with a towel, washing feet, is our cue, rather than the fanfare, ostrich-plume fans, *sedia gestatoria*, and triple tiara that attended the papacy in the late Middle Ages and the Renaissance, and even into our own time. Yes. But we have always to recall that no single image can ever adequately contain the mysteries of the faith. The barefoot Saint Francis in brown and the glittering Michael in gold are both equally images of something that is true. By the same token, the Church as pauper and servant and the Church as "noble army"—this is how the Te Deum speaks of the martyrs—are both images of the manifold mystery of the Church's life and identity.

That is a long digression to attach to one brief moment in the Mass. But of course it is not really a digression. The liturgy points us to, nay, brings us to such vistas in every one of its parts.

The Eucharistic Prayer continues now, recalling Christ's death, Resurrection, and Ascension; offering his sacrifice to the Father; remembering all the faithful, living and departed; and asking that we ourselves may be counted among that great number whose inheritance is nothing less than eternal life in his presence.

The Great Amen

Then, "Through him, with him, in him, in the unity of the Holy Spirit, all glory and honor is yours, almighty Father, for ever and ever." And we respond, "Amen." So be it. With one word we speak volumes. All the heavenly host, and all the redeemed, and in its own way the entire creation cry Amen! to this attributing of glory and honor to the Father. Hell loathes this Amen. And I, heir to Adam that I am, am not readily disposed to join in. *All* honor and glory is his? Like Lucifer in his foolhardy vanity I would like to accrue some glory to myself. It is called pride, this murmuring and persistent wish of mine, and to unlearn it and to learn to cry Amen! with the angels and saints is the whole work of sanctification in me.

There is a profound sense in which the formula to which we have all just replied Amen bespeaks the entire panoply of the drama of our salvation and, beyond that, of the mystery of the Holy Trinity itself. "Through him, with him, in him, in the unity of the Holy Spirit." *Per ipsum, et cum ipso, et in ipso.* . . . What is glimpsed in those words? Theology itself can scarcely approach the mystery—that it is through, with, and in the Son that glory is to be given to the Father. The words of Scripture bring us again and again up to the outer marches of the mystery: "In the beginning was the Word . . . all things were made through him . . . to him be glory in the church by Christ Jesus . . . then the Son himself will also be subjected to him who put all things under him, that God may be everything to everyone" (Jn 1:1, 3; Eph 3:21; 1 Cor 15:28).

We will never in this life, and perhaps even in the next, penetrate this sense in which all that God "does" is bound up in his Son. The mighty chapters in our own story, namely, creation, redemption, glorification, never permit us to forget the centrality of the Son of God in all that we see God doing. Even the long centuries from Eden to the Annunciation, when the name Jesus was not yet known, strain forward on tiptoe, hastening toward the perfect disclosure of God in Jesus Christ. Every altar ever built, from Abel's to the Tabernacle in the wilderness, to Solomon's temple, held the rumor of the Lamb of God who would take away the sin of the world. The Psalms and the Prophets are redolent of the news, Behold, he comes!

Through him, with him, in him: the Catholic Church has no gospel other than this Gospel of Jesus Christ the Lord, the Savior.

10

Communion Rite

Lord's Prayer

The priest then bids us pray "in the words our Savior gave us". The Our Father is without any doubt the most familiar set of words there is for any Catholic. Because of this, we find that we often reach the end of saying it only to have to admit that our minds have been everywhere but here in this prayer. It easily slips into the category "rote" and, for some people, can be rattled off as though it were mumbo-jumbo. Interestingly enough, the Church would be slow to dismiss such rattlings off too fiercely. For one thing, we mortals scarcely ever grasp the full weight of what we are saying to the Most High. And second, presumably in even the most machinelike rapping-out of the words, there flickers *somewhere* in the recesses of the person repeating it some rag of intention, however fragmentary, that prayer go up to the ears of heaven. The Divine Mercy has a way of attaching far more credit to such rags than we parsimonious souls might grant. Often non-Catholic Christians suspect that the Our Father has become a mere incantation among Catholics. If there is any validity in such a suspicion, then only the Divine Mercy himself can make a judgment. Meanwhile, the liturgy puts this prayer in our mouths day by day.

The saints and doctors of the Church right up to Thomas himself have reflected richly on this prayer. The *Catechism* has an entire section devoted to this prayer. In the Lord's Prayer we have the pattern for all prayer. There is no prayer at all going up from this earth that does not find its blueprint, so to speak, in its words. If we will accustom ourselves to approaching it in this way and will try to make at least one of its requests especially our own each time we repeat it, we will find that not only our prayer but our entire spiritual orientation is clarified, instructed, and enriched.

The Lord's Prayer places before us the hardest part, perhaps, of the Christian agenda: "Forgive us our trespasses as we forgive . . ." It puts one's feet right *in* the fire. "Forgive your brother seventy times seven times." Sometimes it is not for 490 different sins; sometimes it is seventy times seven for the same thing. He trod on my insteps once, and my imagination keeps replaying it—and here I am on Forgive #383.

The words which the priest says at the end of the Lord's Prayer, "Deliver us, Lord, from every evil . . .", help to underscore for us what we have just been asking. They particularly strike the note characteristic of every part of the liturgy, namely, eager expectation of "the coming of our Savior, Jesus Christ". The Second Coming of our Lord is often thought of by Catholics, if they think about it at all, as either something infinitely remote that will probably never really happen, or as the specialty of medieval preachers of doom, or of odd sects who intermittently don robes and climb to mountaintops to greet the returning Savior. But if we will pay attention both to Scripture and the liturgy, we will find that our Lord's return is indeed an event, like the Nativity, the Resurrection, and the Ascension, to be kept front and center in our vision.

Sign of Peace

Following the Doxology ("For the kingdom, the power, and the glory are yours . . ."), the priest, recalling the Lord's words in the fourteenth chapter of John's Gospel, in which he bestowed his own peace on his anxious disciples (it was just before the worst happened), offers this peace to us. "The peace of the Lord be with you always." "And also with you", we respond.

Once more we hear the lovely antiphonality which presides *ubi caritas*—wherever Love is to be found, which certainly ought to be true of us gathered here at the invitation of Love himself. It is a piquant note in this exchange which the liturgy asks of us (we may be bidden at this point to greet each other with "Peace!") that the greeting is to be exchanged, not especially between me and the picked few in the congregation whom I find attractive, sympathetic, or exciting. No. I am to greet *whomever* I find about me. Hmm. Suppose this man on my left here is a great bore? And that person behind me irritates me beyond what can reasonably be asked of one. I seem to have got stuck in a section of the congregation where all the scruffiest and most unlikely types have settled. Surely . . .

No, says the liturgy. This greeting, found here in this ceremonial setting, is, in fact, what love says to all men, and you who are assisting at the liturgy are given this chance to begin to learn the script of heaven, so to speak. Certainly hell wants nothing of this sort of glad generosity; and everything in you which is timid, or vain, or brittle, or churlish resists it. But here we go: "The peace of the Lord be with *you!*" (Whoever.) Heigh ho. Such daunting exercises the liturgy imposes on us.

But that is heaven unfurled! We are being asked to get into step with the Dance which greets all. As we advance in Charity we find, as we find with every part of the liturgy, that the words become more and more our own and, far from being alarming or jarring, turn out to be a mode of joy.

Breaking of the Bread

In the Agnus Dei (Lamb of God) we address the Savior in the words of the ancient formula, in use in the liturgy since at least the seventh century, which recalls the title ascribed to him by John the Baptist and which itself recalls the words of Isaiah which the Church has always heard as applicable to the Lord, "He was led as a lamb to the slaughter" (cf. Is 53:7).

How can it be that the sacrifice of himself offered by Jesus Christ at Calvary "takes away" our sin? For one thing, what sort of universe is this in which blood sacrifice seems to be required for sin? And beyond that, how can one man's sacrifice be offered "vicariously", that is, for another (let alone for *all* others)?

No one can penetrate to the root of these mysteries. But it is worth noting that all tribes and cultures seem to have been aware that expiation or propitiation must occur to reconcile us mortals with the deity. *Expiation*: not an easy word. It has a rich and manifold meaning, and in order to encompass it all we need to bring into play a whole array of words: to appease; to atone for; to make amends; to purify; to extinguish guilt; to pay the penalty; to make reparation.

This, say Scripture and the Church, is what was achieved at Calvary for us. It is the core of the gospel, really. The "good tidings" of Christmas are that "a savior is born to you". Light has come (*lux effulgit*) to us, the people who walked in darkness. What darkness? The darkness, alas, of our sins. The darkness of our separation from the glory of God's presence. Who will bring us back? Who will make things right? Who will atone for our sins? The cry goes up from all heathen altars. Every lamb or ox or turtledove whose blood has ever been poured out in any ritual sacrifice testifies to the awareness, at the very depths of the human heart, that expiation must be made if we are to make contact with the deity. (Some deities, Moloch, for example, demanded human sacrifice: a horror, of course; but in its own ghastly and distorted way a testimony to what, at bottom, we fear must happen.) The Christian gospel says, "Good news! The Lamb has been offered. His name is Jesus Christ the Savior."

It is this which we enact in the Mass, and it is this which resounds in the words of the Agnus Dei.

In the repetition of "Have mercy on us" we hear not the anxious or desperate supplication of thralls plucking at the garment of a majesty of which they are in terror (an outsider, especially a modern one, might think he heard some such note in this formula); rather, we hear the Christian voice gladly acknowledging that it is indeed in this mercy so abundantly poured out on us in the Gospel that we stand, now and always. (The "Grant us peace" with which the hymn ends seems to have been inserted in the liturgy during an especially perilous time, but it turns out to be perennially apt. When, one might ask, do we ever find ourselves in a time when such a petition is *not* apt? Every human soul will testify that interior peace is always what we need, even in the all-too-rare moments when no war is raging on the exterior front.)

The title "Lamb of God" is particularly significant at just this moment in the liturgy, the "fraction": While we repeat "Lamb of God", we see the priest raise the Host, break it in half, and place a small fragment in the cup with these words: "May this mingling of the body and blood of our Lord Jesus Christ bring eternal life to us who receive it."

The Host is broken. Why? Because it was the Body of our Lord Jesus Christ *broken* for us on the Cross that is our salvation. At the Last Supper he broke the bread, saying that it was his Body "broken for you". And it is the Blood of our Lord Jesus Christ *poured out* that is our salvation. When his Body was pierced with the nails and then with the spear, his Blood was shed. This word, shed, is included in the various versions of the Eucharistic Prayer: "Shed for you and for all", says the Lord. *For you:* expiation; atonement.

We are in the midst of mysteries here which reach to the center of the mystery of God, of man, and of evil. No one can fully grasp them. Fully? No one can begin to grasp them, really. The theologian and the peasant are on the same footing here, as they are at the Nativity. Shepherds *and* wise men kneel.

Communion

Then the priest raises the Host so that all may see it and says, "This is the Lamb of God, who takes away the sins of the world. Happy are those who are called to his supper."

Supper. We thought we were at the Cross. But once more we have it kept before us that the Mass is both sacrifice and feast. The altar is also a table. Mysteries multiplied and compounded! The blackness of Golgotha dispelled by the heavenly invitation to "Take and eat." "Drink this, all of you."

At this point the priest himself and then the other ministers and servers receive the Body and Blood, and the Communion Antiphon is said or sung. This is a brief text, usually from the Psalms, which echoes in some way what is now occurring in the Mass, namely, that God himself comes to us, or that he feeds us, or that our soul's deepest yearning is for him.

The seventeenth-century poet George Herbert wrote a poem which perhaps catches our mixed feelings here. "Love bade me welcome, yet my soul drew back" ("Love III"). We do well to hesitate in the presence of this mighty Sacrifice. And

yet we hear the gracious invitation, Take and eat.
Drink. It is the Lord who speaks these words.

And so we go "up to the altar of God who is the
joy of my youth", as the old Latin rite had it, to
make our Communion. The Church, we may recall here, urges us to do this frequently. The Mass
is not primarily something to be heard (people
used to speak of "hearing Mass"). It is certainly
legitimate, of course, to be present at Mass and, for
good reason, to refrain from making one's Communion. But this ought not to be our ordinary
routine. We are bidden to the Table.

"The Body of Christ", we hear as we receive
the Host from the priest. "The Blood of Christ",
if the chalice is offered. (The Church teaches that
we receive the whole Christ under each species.
We have not been "half fed" at a Mass where only
the Host is offered.)

In this action we find ourselves at a point not
altogether unlike the great mysteries of birth and
death. That is, we enact, or undergo, what seems
on the surface to be a wholly physical event. But
immense mysteries attend the event. The baby
appears: very physical; but we know that a new
person with an everlasting destiny is now among
us. Or, in the case of death: breathing ceases; the
heart stops; the brain waves go flat. It can all be

charted by the machines. But this scarcely approaches the full import of the event. A soul has gone on its way, out of time, out of its earthly identity, to its destiny, either glory or perdition. Our imaginations fail.

So it is when we "make our communion". The Church teaches that in this act we are made partakers of the life of God himself. If we do not eat the Flesh of the Son of God, and drink his Blood, says our Lord in John 6, we have no life in us. How it can be that this wafer "communicates" to us the life of God is as impenetrable a mystery as birth and death. Nay, it is infinitely greater, since it is not only our own souls at stake in the transaction: Almighty God himself comes to us. Somehow this wafer, which presently dissolves on our tongue, is Jesus, the "Bread of Heaven", the pledge of eternal life. It is not magic: it is sacrament (mystery). An old quatrain touches on what our imaginations fail to grasp:

> His was the word that spake it:
> He took the Bread and brake it;
> And what His word did make it—
> That I believe, and take it.

Perhaps here we see as clearly as may be seen the answer to the charge of some unbelievers that

Christians are hypocritical when they go to church, as though they were some special, privileged elite which is better than ordinary mortals. No. If there is anything in the mind of a Catholic at Mass, it is, "Lord, have mercy on me a sinner", and "Lord, I am not worthy that thou shouldest come under my roof: but speak the word only, and my soul shall be healed."

II

Concluding Rite

Suddenly the Mass ends. One might have thought that, with such a holy rite, it would be fitting to append a number of observances to assist us in making the transition from the Holy of Holies, as it were, back out into the workaday world.

But no. Only the briefest actions send us out. The vessels on the altar are cleansed and arranged, a brief prayer is said, we are greeted ("The Lord be with you"), the priest pronounces the blessing over us, and then we hear "Go."

An onlooker might think it all a bit peremptory. But the faithful know that this is the whole point. What we have done here is to preside over and inform, nay suffuse, our whole week. We may recall how Saint Matthew pictures the Last Supper: immediately after they had shared the bread and the cup he has, "And when they had sung a hymn, they went out" (Mt 26:30). Having been nourished by the Lord's own Body and Blood, we move out to take up the next thing. (The disciples did not do very well in this matter, as it happens; we pray that we do better.)

The Christian liturgy draws us deeper and deeper into the innermost recesses of mystery, but then lands us back out on the street. We are not allowed to stay at the altar. We have to go back out to committee meetings, traffic jams, laundry, dirty diapers—where we will be enacting what we have encountered in the liturgy.

And the dismissal is sweetened, so to speak, in that what sends us out is not the mere monosyllable, Go. It is "Go in peace to love and serve the Lord."

Peace. The infallible recipe for peace between me and my neighbor, or among nations, is the attitude which the Lord himself has taught us and showed us in the entire liturgy, namely, "My life for yours." If I am laying down my life for my neighbor as Jesus Christ laid down his for me, I will not be attacking or quarreling with my neighbor. "Let this mind be in you which was also in Christ Jesus", says Saint Paul. He "emptied himself, and took upon him the form of a servant". If this mind is at work in me and in you, then peace will reign between us.

Go in peace, says the Mass. *Ite, missa est.* We have come full circle in our discussion. Go. The Mass is finished. Take all of this with you as you go.

Recommended Reading

Guardini, Romano. *Meditations before Mass.* Manchester, N.H.: Sophia Institute Press, 1994.

Howard, Thomas. *Chance or the Dance?* San Francisco: Ignatius Press, 1989.

———. *Hallowed Be This House.* San Francisco: Ignatius Press, 1979.

———. *On Being Catholic.* San Francisco: Ignatius Press, 1997.

Pieper, Josef. *Leisure, the Basis of Culture.* New York: New American Library, 1963.

Schmemann, Alexander. *For the Life of the World.* New York: Saint Vladimir's Seminary Press, 1973.

von Hildebrand, Dietrich. *Liturgy and Personality.* Manchester, N.H.: Sophia Institute Press, 1993.